Living with Cancer
With Hope amid the Uncertainty

edited by

PAUL D'ALTON

UNIVERSITY COLLEGE DUBLIN PRESS

PREAS CHOLÁISTE OLLSCOILE
BHAILE ÁTHA CLIATH

2021

First published 2021
by University College Dublin Press
UCD Humanities Institute
Belfield
Dublin 4
Ireland

www.ucdpress.ie

ISBN 978-1-910820-86-5 pb

Cataloguing in Publication data available from the British Library

*The right of Paul D'Alton to be identified as the
author of this work has been asserted by him*

Typeset in Scotland in Plantin and Fournier by Ryan Shiels
Text design by Lyn Davies
Printed on acid-free paper by Bell & Bain Ltd,
Glasgow, G46 7UQ, UK

Contents

Acknowledgements

This book has been in gestation for almost ten years and was written over the final three years of that period. There are many people who encouraged, nurtured, and shaped the book you hold in your hands right now.

First and foremost, I would like to acknowledge and thank the people with cancer I have had the privilege of working with over many years. You have been my real teachers. I would also like to thank: the late beloved and brilliant Dr Jimmie Holland who changed cancer care globally and locally provided great encouragement at the outset of this project; the twelve authors who wrote chapters for this edited collection, it's been a pleasure to work with such kind, generous and experienced folk; my colleagues at the School of Psychology UCD and at St Vincent's University Hospital for their unconditional support over many years, for giving the space and warm collegiality that nurtured this book; UCD Press, in particular Noelle Moran for her encouragement and enthusiasm and her team: Conor Graham in Editorial, Ryan Shiels, Daniel Morehead, Jane Rogers and Cormac Kinsella on publicity; my family and friends who have listened to me for years bemoaning the absence of a book like this and then listened and supported me for three years as we compiled it.

Finally, to Des, without whom this and so many other life projects would never have come to life.

PAUL D'ALTON
Dublin
September 2021

Additional acknowledgements to the following photographers (on Unsplash): Luke Marshall, Steve Johnson, Timothy Eberly, Matias N. Reyes, Markus Spiske, Motoki Tonn, Jan Fillem, Mark Dalton, Conor Luddy, Isham Fernandez, Tim Mossholder, Adam Strong, Clem Onojeghuo.

'Let everything happen to you. Beauty and terror. Just keep going. No feeling is final'

Rainer Maria Rilke

Introduction: How to approach this book

You probably have this book in your hand because you have been diagnosed with cancer and your world has been turned upside down. Or perhaps the dust is beginning to settle after your treatment, and you are trying to find your way in a changed body and a world that feels very different.

Cancer is not just a physical illness; it has an emotional impact that for many can feel scary, unfamiliar, disconcerting and, at times, overwhelming. Sometimes the deluge of information available about the emotional aspects of cancer can ironically also be overwhelming; it can be hard to know what to trust and where to start.

We wrote *Living with Cancer: With Hope amid the Uncertainty* so that you would have reliable, jargon-free, evidence-based information to help guide you through the new and sometimes challenging emotional territory cancer throws us into. It is our hope that this book will provide some hope, help, and comfort in this unfamiliar upside-down world you might find yourself in. Our aim is to help you find your feet again by offering a few signposts, maybe a beacon or two of hope, and plenty of practical information.

When it comes to finding our feet and getting some emotional stability back after a cancer diagnosis one of the most important things to do is to find and put words on our emotional experience. Simply finding words that describe what we experience, and the knowledge that many other people have felt like this, can be a powerful antidote to the overwhelm that a traumatic event like receiving a cancer diagnosis can bring. We hope *Living with Cancer* will help you find words to put to your emotional experience and reassure you that what you are experiencing many other people are going through also.

This book is not necessarily meant to be read from cover to cover. You will see from the chapter titles that this book covers a wide range of issues, some of which will be relevant to you at different times over the course of your treatment and recovery, while others may not be relevant to you at all. So, our invitation is to take what you need from these pages ahead. It might be more of a 'dip in' and 'dip out of' book depending on what works best for you, what you feel able for, and what you are drawn to. Perhaps choose a chapter and make yourself a cup of tea, have a read and then put these pages down. Go with small bite size pieces and go at the pace that feels right for you. You will see that at the end of each chapter there is a list of resources such as books, audiobooks, podcasts, and websites. These resources are offered as a guide for delving further into topics that are of importance for you.

Whilst *Living with Cancer* is primarily written for you – the person who has cancer – it might also be helpful for family members, friends, and loved ones. You may want to share a specific chapter of this book with a family member or a friend so they can better understand your experience.

We hope these pages ahead will be a kind companion to you over the time to come. So, dip in and out, put it back on the shelf, go back to it when you need to, give it to someone else when the time feels right. Go as gently as you can in this new, daunting, and unfamiliar world: you will find your feet, with hope amid the uncertainty.

It is to be noted that all case studies are fictional or a composite of patient stories throughout the text.

PAUL D'ALTON
September 2021

Foreword

While we delight in the extraordinary improvements which have occurred in cancer treatment over the last few decades, the 'burden' of cancer for individual patients who are living with the disease, their families and society at large remains immense, and is arguably growing. How is this? In the first instance, cancer will get more common as populations grow and age. Furthermore, those improvements which have occurred across the spectrum of malignancy, and which have produced increased cure rates in some cancers, meaningful prolongation of survival in many, and more limited benefits in others, have themselves presented new challenges.

There are an ever-increasing number of people who have 'survived cancer' and who are 'living with cancer'. To paraphrase Marcia Smith, cancer 'the death sentence' has been replaced in many cases by cancer the 'life sentence'. The definition of this life sentence has changed for many patients. While it was intended as an exhortation to cancer patients to live their life as fully as possible, the many patients who are now achieving very prolonged survival, frequently experience varying life-long burdens consequent to the disease and its treatment.

Cancer imposes different lives on patients. Some return to near normality, with only the memories of the time on treatment. Others live with the sequelae of life changing side effects of the disease and its treatment. For many others who are enjoying good physical health, concern about the risk of recurrence is ever-present. For all however, those who are cured and those who are not, cancer is a life changing event.

It must also be remembered that it is not just cancer patients who are 'living with cancer', it is also those with whom they share their lives, those who support them. Health care professionals sometimes forget that the rest of life goes on for people who are living with cancer. In many cases, wages have to be earned, families supported, children educated, and relationships maintained and nurtured. Most if not all cancer patients will require additional physical, emotional, and practical support to help them. *Living with Cancer: With Hope amid the Uncertainty* addresses these themes carefully, and by drawing on the experience and expertise of patients and professionals, provides practical and compassionate advice for those who are facing the disease, and their families and carers.

While the book is aimed at individuals, it is to be hoped that policy makers will also read and take note of the lessons it contains. Society and in particular health systems will have to come to grips with the reality that increasing numbers of living cancer patients and survivors will require formalised support. Deficiencies in child-care, home help, community palliative systems and other supports for cancer patients need a much higher priority than they have now in most societies.

This book also correctly emphasises the importance of understanding the psychological burdens of cancer, and the need for expert support. This is an area where substantial development is needed. Our success in treating the disease must not let cancer survivors become another marginalised and structurally disadvantaged group.

Living with Cancer was written during the COVID-19 crisis. As in so many other areas of society, the pandemic has highlighted the special situation of cancer patients and survivors, and the deficiencies and inequalities in the supports that are available to them. The feelings of fear and isolation that so many people experienced during the pandemic were particularly troubling for cancer patients and survivors given their awareness of their heightened vulnerability to the illness. Hopefully the more general debate about equity in health and social care which COVID precipitated, will also prompt attempts to improve the support for cancer patients.

Living with Cancer should also be read by health care professionals who deal with cancer patients. It will provide a wake-up call to those of us who think that all progress in cancer care is always measured in survival curves.

The problem isn't always fixed, even when it seems to be fixed.

PROFESSOR JOHN CROWN

Authors' Biographies

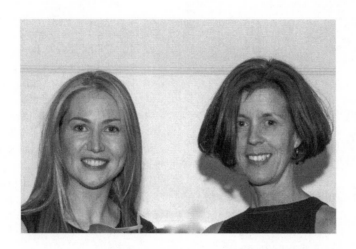

Dr Sonya Collier & Professor Anne-Marie O'Dwyer

Dr Sonya Collier is a Principal Clinical Psychologist in the Psychological Medicine Service, in St James's Hospital, Dublin. She is also an Adjunct Assistant Professor in Trinity College Dublin. Professor Anne-Marie O'Dwyer is a Consultant in Liaison Psychiatry in St James's Hospital Dublin, and Clinical Professor in the School of Medicine in Trinity College Dublin. Together they established the first multi-disciplinary Psycho-Oncology Service in Ireland in 2004. They have published psycho-oncology articles in several peer-reviewed journals and have authored the award-winning self-help manual 'Understanding and Managing Cancer Related Fatigue: A Self-Help Programme Using Cognitive Behavioural Strategies'. Their clinical and research interests are in the development of psychological interventions for alleviating distress caused by cancer and/or its treatment, and in the training of health care professionals working in cancer care.

Orla Crowe

Orla Crowe lives in Dublin, with her husband and two sons. Her pastimes include rambling walks along the coast near her home, meeting with friends and a newly discovered pleasure in gardening. She also loves all that books have to offer. This love grew when she returned to education as a mature student, after having cancer. Since graduating from Trinity College Dublin as a Social Worker, Orla continues to be involved in the education and training of social work students at the School of Social Work and Social Policy at TCD. Orla has a long background in advocating for the rights of people with disabilities and more recently, in the domain of psycho-social support for cancer patients. Orla currently works part-time as a Medical Social Worker in a Dublin teaching hospital.

Dr Paul D'Alton

Dr Paul D'Alton is Head of the Department of Psychology at St Vincent's University Hospital, Dublin and Associate Professor at the School of Psychology, University College Dublin. He has worked in cancer care for almost 15 years. Paul completed his clinical psychology training in Trinity College Dublin in 2004 and has worked as a clinical psychologist, educator, and researcher since then. Paul has completed a number of funded research projects and is frequently invited to speak at national and international scientific gatherings. He has published several book chapters and peer-reviewed journal articles.

Dr Natalie Hession

Dr Natalie Hession is Head of Psycho-oncology Services at St Luke's Radiation Oncology Network. She also is a Research Fellow (School of Psychology) and Adjunct Honorary Professor (School of Nursing) in Trinity College Dublin. She has worked in the area of Psycho-oncology and cancer care for 17 years, where she manages the service and provides clinical assessment and therapeutic intervention for individuals and families in relation to all aspects of the psychological impact of cancer. Dr Hession has a track record for being committed to the development of Psycho-oncology in Ireland and has contributed by way of policy development and media coverage. She lectures, trains, supervises research, has made many professional presentations nationally and internationally, as well as publishing widely in the area of Psycho-oncology.

Professor Michaela J. Higgins

Michaela J. Higgins is a Consultant Medical Oncologist at St Vincent's University Hospital, Dublin, and a Clinical Professor at University College Dublin (UCD). Professor Higgins previously worked as a Consultant Oncologist in Massachusetts General Hospital, Boston and the Mater Misericordiae University Hospital, Dublin. She specialises in the care of patients with breast cancer and has published extensively in this area. She has been involved in active clinical cancer research for the past 10 years and has received multiple competitive grants and awards. Professor Higgins regularly teaches undergraduates at UCD and young doctors in training.

Dr Tara Kingston

Dr Tara Kingston is a Liaison Psychiatry Consultant in St James's Hospital in Dublin, where she is Clinical Lead in the Psychological Medicine Service. She is Senior Clinical Lecturer in Psychiatry at Trinity College Dublin. Dr Kingston has been working clinically in the area of Psycho-oncology since 2014. She has qualifications in Cognitive Behaviour Therapy and has also trained in Group Analytic Psycho-therapy. She has a special interest in the use of Mindfulness in both Psycho-oncology and Depression, having worked clinically and published research in these areas.

Dr Siobhan McHale

Dr Siobhan MacHale is a Consultant Liaison Psychiatrist in Beaumont Hospital and Associate Professor in The Royal College of Surgeons of Ireland. She trained as a physician before specialising in Psychiatry. She is a member of the NCCP National Psycho-Oncology Advisory Group and has been involved in the care of patients in both Cancer and Palliative Care settings in her role as a Consultant Liaison Psychiatrist for over 20 years. She greatly values multidisciplinary team working and has always been fascinated by the art and language of mind-body medicine.

Professor Louise McHugh

Professor Louise McHugh works in the School of Psychology at University College Dublin. She is the director of a research lab called the Contextual Behavioural Science lab, and for the past 20 years she has been researching a psychological intervention recommended for long-term conditions called Acceptance and Commitment Therapy. She has written over 100 academic papers and two books on the topic. Louise lives in Dublin, is a long-suffering Mayo supporter and a budding improv comedian.

Dr Caoimhe McLoughlin

Dr Caoimhe McLoughlin completed her specialist training in Consultant-Liaison Psychiatry, the branch of medicine that focuses on the care of patients with co-occurring medical and mental health conditions. In addition to publishing in this area, she has a master's degree in Psychoanalytic Psycho-therapy from Trinity College Dublin, a Professional Diploma in Clinical Leadership from RCSI, and is a member of the Euro-pean Association of Psychosomatic Medicine. She is currently based in the Royal Infirmary Hospital, Edinburgh having been awarded a place on the European ETUDE PhD Fellowship Programme for Functional Disorders, a group of conditions that lie on the interface of psychiatry and medicine.

Dr Susan Moore

Dr Susan Moore is Consultant Liaison Psychiatrist in St Vincent's University Hospital, Dublin. She undertook a fellowship at the Institute of Psychiatry, Psychology and Neuroscience and Maudsley Hospital in London and has collaborated on research focusing on the interface between physical and mental health. She has worked in the field of Psych-oncology since 2014.

Mary Moriarty

Mary Moriarty holds a number of roles as part of her work with the Psycho-oncology Service at St Vincents University Hospital, Dublin. Prior to working as a Clinical Nurse Specialist in Psycho-oncology Mary worked as a Mental Health Nurse, General Nurse, Midwife, Lymphoedema and Complementary Therapist. She is also a qualified Systemic Psychotherapist. Mary works with both in-patients and out-patients of the hospital at the time of diagnosis, during treatment, into survivorship and at end of life. Mary completed her Masters in Systemic Psychotherapy between the School of Medicine UCD and The Mater Family Therapy Programme in 2017. Her research thesis focused on the experience of parents of young adults and adolescents with cancer.

Dr Louise O'Driscoll

Dr Louise O'Driscoll is a Senior Clinical Psychologist in Psycho-oncology at St Vincent's University Hospital, Dublin having worked in the area of cancer care since 2008. She is passionate about improving the experience of cancer patients and their loved ones. This motivation drives her commitment to clinical work, research, teaching, and service development. She has published and presented research nationally and internationally and teaches on several postgraduate programmes. Most recently Louise has been granted funding from the Irish Cancer Society to co-lead a national project into the needs of individuals with a high genetic risk of cancer. She was a member of a psychology team who contributed to the 2017–27 National Cancer Strategy, the first to explicitly mandate the psychological needs of patients. She serves on the Irish Psycho-social Oncology Network Research Steering Group and has previously served on the Organising Committee for the 2016 International Psycho-oncology Society World Congress and on the St Vincent's University Hospital Medical Research and Ethics Committee. In her most important role, Louise is a mum who believes in the innate resilience of parents and children, and it is her privilege to support families in her work.

Dr Susan O'Flanagan

Dr Susan O' Flanagan is a Senior Clinical Psychologist who works at St Vincents University Hospital, Dublin. Susan provides clinical psychology services to adults living with a range of chronic illnesses and has a wealth of experience in working with people affected by cancer. Susan completed her Doctorate in Clinical Psychology at NUI Galway, and prior to this she undertook a health psychology masters and a research masters in the area of

bereavement. Susan has a keen interest in research and teaching and has presented at international conferences, published in peer-reviewed academic journals, and contributes to teaching at undergraduate and postgraduate level. Since completing her doctorate Susan has completed formal training in a wide range of psychotherapeutic approaches with a strong emphasis on mindfulness-based and compassion-focused therapies. Susan works in an integrative, individualised, and collaborative way with patients to best support them to adapt to and live with long-term health conditions and the changes to function, identity, and relationships they can pose. In particular, she is passionate about opening conversations and discussing important challenges that often remain silent in cancer care, such as the impact of illness and treatment on appearance and sexual functioning.

Dr David Shannon

Dr David Shannon is Senior Chartered Counselling Psychologist at Our Lady's Hospice and Care Services in Dublin. He has worked in Palliative Care for ten years and also in the area of cancer care for four years. David feels privileged to work with patients in their own homes and across in-patient hospice settings at all stages of advanced illness. He has developed a special interest in the role of mindfulness meditation for people receiving palliative care. David is also part of the core training team at Bangor University's (North Wales) Centre for Mindfulness Research and Practice, and regularly trains and supervises others to teach mindfulness.

CHAPTER I

Patient voice

Orla Crowe

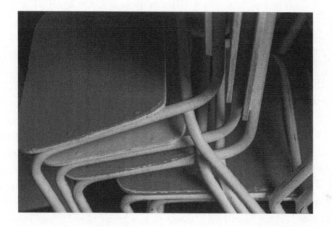

Life is amazing. And then it's awful. And then it's amazing again. And in between the amazing and awful it's ordinary and mundane and routine. . . that's just living, heart-breaking, soul-healing, amazing, awful, ordinary life. And it's breathtakingly beautiful.

– L. R. Knost

The day of our son's Christmas concert was one of those beautiful, crisp December mornings. It was also the day after I was diagnosed with cancer. My husband and sister were the only two people who knew. I hadn't said it out loud yet because then it would be real and there would be no going back.

The atmosphere was festive as we stood jammed among the crowd outside the school hall. When the doors opened at ten on the button, I could hear the echoey sounds of stampeding footsteps, galloping to the front to nab the best seats. The concert began in all its Christmassy cheer, exhibiting the usual array of tea towels secured from kitchens, then sellotaped carefully onto small heads.

I

Watching my son on stage, a little bashful, singing along with all the other little people, fearing his innocence might soon be broken by my illness, was heart breaking. After a while he spotted me, his face lit up and he beamed a wide, proud, open smile. At the sight of him, my body almost folded in on itself with poignancy. My heart bursting with love for my boy wondering if I would be here next Christmas.

As the concert ended, the clatter of the chairs being piled away before people were barely out of them, brought home to me the certainty that the world keeps on turning; no matter what. It felt surreal. My life, once so familiar and solid, was now unrecognisable. What I could not have known then, was that recognising myself as a 'cancer patient' would soon become the new familiar, making life a little less scary – scary but manageable. Nevertheless, the process of getting to that point required time.

By its nature cancer is an ambiguous, shocking, and frightening life experience which brought up disconcerting feelings of fear, anger, and helplessness. I had no control over the disease that was already inside my body; no hoping or wishing would change that. The only thing I had control over was my response to it.

It seemed logical to focus my attention on things that *were* within my control. Or maybe it wasn't logical at all, maybe this was just my way of coping. Whatever it was, I realise now it was my attempt to feel less powerless.

I focused on small things which I could achieve. For example, as inconsequential as it may sound, I decided that no matter how desperate I felt, I would have a shower every single day. This might not sound too ambitious but there were times during the cycle of the treatment, when even having a simple shower was a difficult feat. Even as I write this, I feel a sense of accomplishment that I managed to achieve that goal.

My perception of 'time' also impacted my ability to manage my situation. Previously, time was marked by numbers on a clock and dates on a calendar. I took time for granted. I held an unconscious assumption: there's plenty more where that came from. I won't make that mistake again.

Time passes: one of the few things guaranteed in life. When a cancer diagnosis has been received time can be your friend and your foe. At stages of my treatment, the idea of time stretching endlessly in front of me, feeling as I did, was excruciating. As I lurched from one anti-sickness tablet to the next, I could bear to look no further than the next few hours. Contemplating time in small bite size chunks was all I could do: an innate survival instinct, perhaps. Looking back, I believe that being able to shape time into manageable portions, by not looking too far ahead, helped me cope with how difficult things were in that moment.

As the symptoms eased between the cycles of chemo, I began to feel better in myself. Because I was feeling less unwell, hope bubbled up enabling me to look beyond the here and now to future events. Now, the idea of time stretching endlessly in front of me was delightful. I especially recall imagining future family holidays (hot sun warming my back; bare feet planted into cool sand; rhythmic sound of waves crashing: sheer bliss). I might have been clinging to a future – any future. Whatever the logic, it felt encouraging to feel this way and gave me hope that one day I would be back on that beach again, in the company of the people who matter.

So, there I was, on the cusp of an unknown future with few promises, or tidy guarantees. Those few sentences from a doctor and everything I knew was snatched away. With scary, crystal clarity, my changed life was laid out in front of me in all its bald reality. The torturous thought of leaving the ones I love was the most painful. Having cancer really brings into sharp awareness the tenderness of life.

In not turning away from what was happening to me, a process of 'allowing' began. Cancer does not go away of its own accord, so I had to face it. I think this allowing came by painfully contemplating the worst-case scenario – death – usually during the night as sleep escaped me, then coming back from that thought to actual reality: I'm alive now.

A tentative coming to terms with having cancer parallel with not trying to make things better or different, gave me a new way to relate to this brutal life event. I found I was able to face the torment of it without being destroyed by the torment of it. A deep knowing from the heart, I think, rather than the brain. From this broader awareness – a psychological ground zero of sorts – came a freedom, an opening, giving me choices.

With my life so suddenly and abruptly derailed, I returned to the question posed by the poet Mary Oliver 'Tell me, what is it you plan to do with your one wild and precious life?' Now, I could choose to fully immerse myself in this difficult, precious, and fragile life: feel the fear, take risks, maybe even kick up my heels. Alternatively, I could live the rest of my life focusing on the fear, forever afraid of what I might lose, and all that might go wrong. That was my choice.

Paradoxical as it sounds, surrendering to the reality of having cancer somehow made the experience easier to cope with. It gave me the emotional space to find meaning in what I was going through. My personal meaning came with the acceptance that I was the 'one' in the one-in-two of us who will get cancer over our lifetime. Nothing different or special about me. Put simply, cancer was to be one of my life experiences. I must say that I feel enormous gratitude that this was not to be my final life experience; I made it out the other side. I know everyone is not so lucky.

The waiting never ends. It can be unbearable at times. Waiting for scans, surgery, appointments, bad news, good news, time to go fast, time to go slow, the next chemo, the final chemo, and then what? So, you can imagine how any break in the waiting is greeted like a welcome friend. One such break came in the form of a new fish tank for the (literal) waiting room of the oncology ward. But before that, a fellow patient and myself struck up what I would call a 'real' conversation. Having cancer made me vulnerable and I think it is accurate to say that he and I might have recognised something in each other – trepidation maybe. As complete strangers, we took a leap of faith in the comfort of human connection and plunged right in and spoke to each other straight from the heart. We spoke of all the waiting, and then of our fear, and our never-ending love for our children and the agonising thought of leaving them. I think there is something precious and profound about authentic conversations which inexplicably offer comfort long after-wards. I suspect 'real' conversations like this are taking place in wards and waiting rooms up and down the country. Not that any of us would choose this yet being surrounded by fellow patients does help normalise the experience. We tend to cope better with things that feel normal to us.

A momentary observation and interaction a little later reminded me of the nurturing value of humour and, for me, as an indicator of normality: a nod to the 'Orla-before-cancer'. Let me explain. Just as he and I finished talking, a ginormous fish tank was wheeled to the door of the waiting room by two workmen. I was fascinated to see how this huge tank with the sloshing, slightly startled looking fish would be maneuvered into place. The potential for calamity was high, so with slight trepidation and I must admit, some amusement, we settled in to watch the theatre unfold. After whispered consultation, the tank was half-shouldered and half-lifted over the threshold. One more heave ho – it's in. It almost called for a round of applause. After all that sloshing, I'd say the fish were more nauseous than the whole waiting room of cancer patients put together!

Then, with a twinkle in his eye and without moving a muscle my companion said: 'It'll take a bit more than goldfish to de-stress us.' We locked eyes then burst out laughing. That fleeting, uplifting moment presented itself: we could have missed it. Relieving pressure, distracting ourselves, who cares, it sure felt good to laugh! Cancer or not – I was still me, delighted to feel 'normal' again: whatever normal is. What I took from this was the knowledge that enriching life experiences just like 'The Waiting Room moments' are happening all around. They help contextualise the unbearable moments.

Although cancer is a disease of the individual its effects ripple out to the entire family and beyond. The experience is a different one for those who love us. It is hard for them too. In the darker moments, again, usually during the night, I wondered how my little family would manage if I was not here. My dear husband is wondering the same thing.

There is no right or wrong way to do this. You are the expert in your own life, only you know what makes your family tick and now is the time to pull together and work as a unit. That means saying yes to the offers of driving, form filling, shopping, bringing the pragmatic one to key medical appointments, and so on.

Next, I share my parenting experience as one example of the tendrils of cancer into family life. Without words ever being spoken, children sense the changed atmosphere. You know your own child best so do whatever you think is right for *them*. Then trust yourself. I worried enormously about the children. Making plans to cater to their separate needs consumed enormous energy and focus.

An instance with my younger son, later in the process, proved I need not have worried quite so much. With the chemo behind me and the tranche of daily radio therapy sessions beginning, my son was curious about where I was going every day. He was asking lots of questions. After careful consideration, I decided to consult with the hospital staff to investigate if he could come along with me some day. My intention was to demystify where I was going and what happened when I got there. When the preparations were in place I asked him, with a forced nonchalance, if he would like to come along with me some day. A sincere 'ok' from him sealed the deal. The relevant staff were advised of the impending arrival of my little VIP. From the minute we stepped through the doors, he was warmly welcomed by name (so important) and made a bit of a fuss of: I really appreciated that.

Besides the sweets from the vending machine, what made my son's visit a success was not the pristine environment, although that helps, or the wonders of modern medicine, it was the opportunity for him to see for himself that this was just another hospital, only nicer than the children's hospitals where we were regulars. We sat; my name was called; he waited; I met the doctor; and then we left. What equally made it a success was the recognition he received on arrival, the feeling of welcome – much overlooked for young and old, if you ask me. Having seen all this with his own eyes meant the mystery was gone for him now and that was the end of the questions.

I share this anecdote to give a realistic sense of how the children adapted. Ensuring our children could tolerate our changed lives was the single most important thing in my world at that time. For them, the indicators of those changes, such as my regular hospital attendance eventually became utter non-events. In retrospect, I could have had more faith in them as individuals. Maybe children *are* more resilient than we give them credit for. It has been my experience, if this helps at all, that the truth is best: accurate, age-appropriate information, shared early and updated as needed. Little or lesser communication with children does not equate to less anxiety for them.

Driven by enduring love, I did the best I could for them. I worried about an imagined future and the impact my cancer would have on their sense of security. But maybe that's what parents and others do in this situation – that must be ok too. None of us want our children's imagination to run wild at this time or for them to worry unnecessarily. They are too precious for that. Although it is hard on the heart, honest and considered communication may aid their coping. A little easier to say than do, but worth it in the long run.

From the third-floor oncology ward, a familiar shopping centre with its distinct purple and turquoise sign lay in my line of vision. As I sat in one of the red treatment chairs waiting for the chemo to sludge into my veins, my mind wandered. I imagined all the people inside, milling around doing ordinary things and wished I was one of them. I longed for a life of ordinariness. When the treatment was all over for me, I headed back to that shopping centre like a necessary pilgrimage, but with cake and coffee as my final reward. As I sipped my coffee, I recalled the vivid image of the red treatment chairs with today's patients in them: almost like a mirror image looking back at me. Here I was – full circle – never believing that when I was sitting in the red treatment chair, I could be the ordinary one again.

Then I thought of equivalent chairs in all the other hospitals, willing their occupants peace and calm as they navigated this excruciatingly uncertain phase of their life. A gush of gratitude washed over me, knowing timing and medical expertise came together in perfect harmony, allowing me to make it out the other side of cancer. I wish it was this way for all of us.

When you are in the thick of it, you might feel supported knowing a relentlessly dedicated group of people are working tirelessly to make this harrowing experience as good as it can be. You are not on your own in this. The kindness of others, strangers and not, has touched me deeply and left an imprint on my life.

It must be acknowledged that cancer also brings with it, tremendous loss: life, dreams, capacity, identity, the possibility of parenthood, and so much more. Loss which is personal and unique to each one of us; every loss deserving to be acknowledged. Parallel to that or maybe because of that, a different way of seeing life filters through.

It is natural to be curious about your cancer and all available treatment options. Your medical team know you best and are the primary point of contact for heath information and advice; they will propose the best treatment plan for you.

The use of technology has become an integral part of how we communicate, all the same, inaccurate, unscientific, and unsolicited online advice has the potential to cause unnecessary distress. Limiting your social media usage to official recommended forums might avoid overstimulating an already overactive mind or going down an information rabbit hole. This can be a difficult enough road without worrying about things that may never happen or spending precious time and energy investigating pseudoscientific treatments.

There is a fine line between staunch independence and allowing yourself to be cared for. In my determination to keep going, I almost did not allow others to show their care for me and my family. What a loss that would have been. Every single act of kindness served as a turbo boost of goodwill, keeping us going when things were really tough.

You may have already been advised to accept all the help you can get. At risk of sounding like an echo: accept all the help you can get. If you are someone who finds support difficult to receive, I would encourage you to gather your courage, close your eyes and allow your muscle memory to form the words: Yes please. It can be difficult to manage even some of the most mundane roles and responsibilities at this time. Letting go of some of that responsibly to others is both pragmatic and nurturing. It offers people a way to show they care. They say it takes a village to raise a child. Maybe it takes a village to carry the sick for a little while too.

For some, the transition back to life after cancer is smooth. For others, the readjustment is not as straightforward as you might expect. Cancer threatens us physically and psychologically. It has the capacity to destroy us physically and psychologically. Thankfully more and more of us are living through our cancer and beyond. What *is* common for many of us though, is a sense of untethered floundering, as we readjust to a life which includes the experience that was cancer.

If you find yourself floundering and could do with a little extra support, please reach out. Expressing how you are feeling to your own network of family and friends may be enough. If not, a tiered range of hospital and community supports are in place, including the network of Cancer Support Centres dotted across the country. They all exist for good reason.

When I look back, I feel incredulous that I managed. What seemed impossible on that crisp December morning as I stood on the steps of the school hall – overwhelmed and afraid of what lay ahead – was not impossible after all. It was not smooth, but with the help of others, I got through.

The finite nature of time and the fragility of being human has changed my view of the world and my place within it. Having cancer gave me a fresh opportunity to give my attention to the things that matter; re-teaching me the importance of some things and the unimportance of others.

Each of us will get through an experience like cancer the best way we can; try not to ask any more from yourself than that.

Whatever your stage of illness, dear reader, I wish you the easiest road and the best of outcomes.

ADDITIONAL RESOURCES

Book:
Irvin D. Yalom, *Staring at the Sun: Overcoming the Terror of Death* (New Jersey, 2010)

Websites:
Irish Cancer Society www.cancer.ie
Marie Keating Foundation www.mariekeating.ie

Other Supports:
Your nearest Cancer Support Centre will provide a range of practical and emotional support such as counselling, entitlements service, support groups along with therapies to promote wellbeing such as art therapy, reflexology, massage, yoga and more.

CHAPTER 2

Cancer: What's it all about?

Michaela J. Higgins

WHAT IS CANCER?

Why is there all this talk about cancer? Well, it's because one in two of us born after 1960 will develop cancer in our lifetime. This means that cancer is very likely to either directly impact each one of us, or someone we love. Happily, many cancers are curable and there are now many more cancer survivors and wider treatment options than ever before.

Cancer starts as a single microscopic cell that cannot be detected by any scan or blood test. Such cells develop from normal healthy tissues but grow in an uncontrolled way. At first cancer cells grow larger within the same area they started from, but unfortunately as they evolve they develop the ability to spread. This is the defining feature of cancer, and this crab-like movement or activity is what gave rise to the term 'cancer'. These abnormal or cancer cells may move to local lymph nodes (also called lymph glands), or they may invade the blood stream and move to other organs within the body: this is called distant metastases.

Cancers may evolve over time and ultimately become resistant or less sensitive to different treatments. This is akin to viruses or bacteria which also change and mutate over time to become resistant to standard antibiotics. Cancer cells can evolve quickly and as they do so, they usually adapt to multiply even more rapidly and continue to grow and divide even if the cells are damaged. When I was a medical student, a great teacher explained to us that 'cancer cells have no shame' – meaning that cancer cells don't die when they ought to.

In our healthy body, normal cells are dividing, growing, and dying in a regular fashion many thousands of times a day. The body has a system of checks and balances in place to make sure that this process happens without error. In a non-cancerous cell, mutant or malfunctioning components are identified and destroyed. Unfortunately, cancer cells develop ways to circumvent these safety checks and continue to multiply and spread even when they are diseased. Fortunately, humans are pretty smart too. In the last few decades our understanding of what causes cancer, how to prevent it, how to detect it early and how to treat it, has significantly deepened leading to much improved outcomes for patients with cancer.

WHY DO SOME OF US GET CANCER AND OTHERS DON'T?

Cancer becomes more common with age. The incidence of cancer in Ireland, for example, is expected to rise greatly as the population of those aged over 65 increases over the coming decades. Life expectancy is rising worldwide due to improvements in social conditions, better prevention and treatment of infectious illnesses, and improved outcomes for cardiovascular disease. The only down-side of an improved life expectancy is that there is a longer period of time and therefore greater opportunity to get cancer.

1. Genetics: Approximately 10–15 per cent of the cancers we see are related to inherited risks, i.e., something about the DNA we inherited from our mother or father that predisposed us to make cancers more than other people in the community. Well described examples of this would be alterations or mutations in the *BRCA1* or *BRCA2* genes which make individuals more likely to form breast, ovarian and rarely other tumours. Knowledge is power in these settings. Individuals with such genetic predispositions can be offered preventative surgery or targeted intensive screening so that future cancers are detected at an early and curable stage

or prevented altogether. Another very common hereditary cancer syndrome would be Lynch syndrome which is associated with abnormalities in the genes that are involved with 'mismatch repair'. (This is one of the checks and balance processes discussed above.) People with defects in these genes are prone to forming cancers of the colon (large bowel) and females are at increased risk of endometrial (womb) and ovarian cancers. Again, there are highly effective screening measures for these families.

2. Environmental: The most common cancer killer in the world is lung cancer and it, and many other cancers such as throat, bladder, and oesophageal cancers, are often directly related to a history of smoking. The single most impactful thing the entire world could do to eradicate hundreds of thousands of cancers every year would be to get the world to give up smoking. Asbestos exposure is now known to be linked to the later development of a rare type of lung cancer called mesothelioma. While asbestos is no longer used in Irish buildings, it is still widely available in other parts of the world.

3. Viruses: Hepatitis B/C, certain strains of the Human Papilloma Virus (HPV) and Ebstein Barr Viruses (EBV) can cause cancers, usually many years after the original exposure. These viruses are endemic in some parts of the world and others can be transmitted with sexual or blood contact. Fortunately, effective immunisation programmes are widely available against most of these harmful viruses and significantly reduce the incidence of pre-cancerous changes and invasive cancer in fully vaccinated individuals. Ireland now has HPV vaccination available for all secondary school children which will prevent the occurrence of many future cervical cancer and head and neck cancers. Countries such as Australia and Canada with well-established HPV vaccination programmes are already seeing significant reductions in the incidence of cancerous cervical changes.

4. Harmful lifestyle habits: Excessive alcohol intake and obesity are also linked to increased cancer diagnoses. It's certainly not always easy but maintaining a healthy body weight and keeping a diet rich in plant-based foods and low in highly processed foods would be beneficial for all of us and would reduce the incidence of many cancers.

5. Unknown: While the cancer community and scientific research has made phenomenal progress in recent decades, we unfortunately cannot fully explain why all cancers develop. It is likely that they are caused by a number of factors coming together including mild genetic predispositions, environmental factors, and lifestyle factors.

PREVENTION IS BETTER THAN CURE, EARLY DETECTION IS ALSO GREAT

Some cancers can be completely prevented by modifying behaviour (e.g., giving up smoking), vaccination against causative viruses or, in individuals with a gene mutation that puts them at high risk of developing cancer, by having prophylactic surgery. Prevention is of course the ideal 'treatment' for cancer, but next best is early detection. The logic here is that the vast majority of cancers are curable if they are identified at an early stage, before they have metastasized (spread to other organs), and some undergo many years of changes before they become fully malignant. This is why several successful screening programmes have been introduced to detect early changes and remove the tissues involved before they become an incurable cancer.

National Screening Services in Ireland

The National Screening Service, now part of the Health Service Executive (HSE), encompasses three national population-based cancer screening programmes:

- BreastCheck: The National Breast Screening Programme
- CervicalCheck: The National Cervical Screening Programme
- BowelScreen: The National Bowel Screening Programme

These programmes aim to reduce morbidity and mortality in the population through early detection of disease and treatment, both of which greatly improve health outcomes. All tests are offered free of charge. A screening test is designed for populations of individuals who do not have any symptoms of disease. It aims to identify those with a risk marker for a disease and ensure early treatment. A screening test is not a diagnostic test, which is designed for individuals with symptoms of a disease or for those identified with a risk marker to assess whether they have it or to follow its progress.

The Breastcheck programme in Ireland invites all women between ages 50 and 69 to take a mammogram every two years. Women and people with a cervix between the age of 25 and 65 should go for regular cervical screening when invited. The BowelScreen colorectal screening programme will offer free screening to men and women aged 55 to 74 on a two-yearly cycle. To develop capacity for the full population, the programme is being implemented on a phased basis, starting with men and women aged 60 to 69.

No screening test is 100 per cent reliable. Always see a GP if you have any concerns or symptoms at any time. More information about the National Screening Services is available at www.screeningservice.ie/

THE MULTIDISCIPLINARY TEAM: WHO'S WHO?

Once a cancer is diagnosed, every patient should have their case reviewed at a multi-disciplinary team (MDT) meeting with a consensus treatment plan agreed. These meetings are held every day of the week in cancer centres around Ireland and include cancer specialists from across many different fields including at a minimum: pathology, radiology, surgery, medical oncology, and radiation oncology.

- Consultant Pathologist: Doctor who examines biopsies (small samples) or larger specimens from body tissues. S/he is also responsible for performing specialist lab tests on specimens that help to reach a diagnosis.
- Consultant Radiologist: Medical doctor who specialises in using medical imaging techniques such as X-rays, CT-scans, or MRI scans.
- Consultant Surgeon: Doctor who performs surgeries or operations.
- Consultant Medical Oncologist: Medical doctor who cares for patients with cancer and provides treatments such as chemotherapy, immunotherapy, or targeted treatments.
- Consultant Radiation Oncologist: Specialist physician who uses ionising radiation in the treatment of cancer.
- Palliative Medicine Consultant: Specialist physician who provides medical care that relieves pain, symptoms, and stress caused by serious illnesses.

The multi-disciplinary team may often also include specialist nurses with expertise in particular cancer types, psychologists, social workers, psychiatrists, research nurses and dieticians.

WHAT TREATMENTS ARE AVAILABLE FOR CANCER?

If a tumour is confined to one area, removing it via an operation/surgery is often the best approach. Some tumours may not need to be removed or it may not be possible to remove them safely. In these situations, a combination of radiotherapy and chemotherapy may be used to shrink the tumours. As a Consultant Medical Oncologist, I look after patients and may offer them different types of 'systemic treatment', which means the medication enters the blood stream and treats cancer cells throughout the body. Systemic treatments include chemotherapy, endocrine treatment, immunotherapy, or targeted treatment (or a careful combination of these).

Chemotherapy

Chemotherapies are medicines (either intravenous or oral) that enter the blood stream and kill cells that are multiplying. In general, cancer cells are multiplying far more rapidly than healthy/normal cells so they are affected most by chemotherapy, but unfortunately chemotherapy has effects on normal cells too and that's why chemotherapy can cause unwanted side effects such as hair loss, nausea, diarrhoea, and an increased risk of infection. Chemotherapy is never given alone. It is given with very sophisticated medications which minimise the potential side effects and is always provided in a cancer centre with specialised staff to support and monitor patients. There are lots of different types and doses of chemotherapy and a medical oncologist will decide with the patient which particular treatment might be best. Each dose is administered only after the patient has been assessed by the team and their blood tests are satisfactory. No two patients on an oncology day ward are receiving the same exact medication, it is in fact highly customised to each individual patient.

Endocrine/Hormonal treatments

The healthy body has several organs which are designed to respond to hormones such as the breast (which can change during pregnancy and periods), the womb, and the prostate. Many cancers which arise in these organs also have hormone receptors on them and are stimulated to grow and multiply by hormones such as oestrogen or testosterone. Medications (often in tablet form) can be given to block the hormones from being produced or block the receptor where they activate the cancer cell. These medicines are very active and powerful in treating cancers and often have less side effects than chemotherapy.

Immunotherapy

Immunotherapy medications try to harness the body's own immune system to attack cancer cells. This group would include drugs called 'checkpoint inhibitors' which take the breaks off the natural systems in the body which prevent destruction of abnormal cells. Usually given intravenously, these medications have shown tremendous activity in some, but unfortunately not all cancers. They have become available in the last five to ten years, and new indications to use them are expanding almost monthly. They are, in general, better tolerated than chemotherapy but can cause problems with hormonal systems in the body such as thyroid, adrenal, or pancreatic abnormalities. They have other rare but serious side effects. Sometimes we use them alone, in other settings they are used in combination with chemotherapy.

Targeted treatments

This term is used to describe oral medicines which target particular genetic abnormalities within the cancer cell, and thus aim to have effects on the cancer cell without too many side effects. Tumour samples are tested to see if they have any 'targetable mutations' in the laboratory, as these drugs only work if a patient's tumour harbours the specific target. Examples would be Osimertinib for EGFR-mutant lung cancer, or Alectinib for ALK-positive lung cancer. Although they can work extremely well, these drugs are suitable only for a minority of patients, and still need to be closely monitored.

Radiotherapy

Radiotherapy is the use of ionising radiation (X-Rays) to treat tumours. Small doses can be given over a series of days or weeks in specialised units. This treatment can be used to reduce the risk of cancer returning after surgery or for relief of pain caused by tumour.

Clinical trials

Nearly all of the treatments we have to offer patients today, and all recent advances, have come about because of the many thousands of patients that participated in clinical trials all over the world. Clinical trials have allowed us to learn better what works and what does not in the treatment of cancers. I believe that patients receive the best possible clinical care by participating in a clinical trial. That said, in order for clinical trial data to be meaningful and the results informative for patients, trials often require patients to meet strict eligibility criteria, i.e., share similar cancer and general health characteristics. Thus, there will not be a clinical trial option available for every patient at every time in their treatment journey. I would recommend that each patient asks their oncologist about whether or not there is a suitable clinical trial option for them, and if interested take a look at what is available on the Clinical Trials Ireland website at www.cancertrials.ie.

Alternative versus complementary care

When I am treating a patient, I care very much about their quality of life. An exceedingly important part of my job is to know when to offer treatment and sometimes to consider when not to offer treatment. The goals of care may be to cure a patient or, in some cases, to relieve symptoms caused by the cancer or, to prolong life. Unfortunately, many of the treatments mentioned above come with the potential for side effects. That is why everything we prescribe should only be done after thoughtful consideration with the patient of the pros and cons.

Many of my patients use complementary therapies such as acupuncture and aromatherapy to ease symptoms from either their cancer or its treatment. I am very supportive of my patients doing something that makes them feel good, such as a lovely day at the beach, a meal with family, a massage, or music therapy.

There is also a dizzying array of alternative therapies available and, for the most part, there is very little robust scientific information to prove that they have true efficacy against cancer and even less information to let us know if they are safe to take by themselves or in combination with standard treatments such as chemotherapy and immunotherapy. When such therapies are being touted as 'cures' and large amounts of money are required for treatment, I am particularly sceptical. Unfortunately, there are many individuals online who have ulterior motives for recommending various therapies to patients.

Products marketed as 'dietary supplements' are not required to undergo the same rigorous testing as medicinal products. The labelling of these products does not meet the same standard as it does for medicines, and it is often hard to tell what exactly is in them. In these cases, I take a very cautious approach as I cannot vouch for their safety.

I would encourage all patients to be honest with their doctor about what products they are using or considering. Doctors and their patients are on the same team. Both want the best possible outcome.

ADDITIONAL RESOURCES

I tell my patients that too much Google can be bad for your health. The management of patients with cancer is increasingly nuanced and requires detailed clinical experience to formulate. The average medical oncologist will have gone to college for six years and trained for a further six to ten years before becoming a consultant. Even with this extensive experience, we often consult with each other to provide the best possible management plans for patients. Be judicious when reading on the internet as every case is different. Two individuals who seemingly have the same cancer might appropriately have distinctly different and tailored treatment plans.

That said, the internet also contains a wealth of helpful and trustworthy information sites. I recommend use of recognised cancer society websites where possible, such as: Irish Cancer Society (www.cancer.ie); Macmillan Cancer Services (www.macmillan.org.uk); American Cancer Society (www.cancer.org); or the European Society for Medical Oncology (www.esmo.org/for-patients), all of which have plenty of accessible information for patients and their families.

CHAPTER 3

Typical emotional reactions to cancer: Four seasons in one day

Paul D'Alton

INTRODUCTION

'I just couldn't believe what the doctor was saying, it felt like a really bad dream', is very often how people describe their first emotional reaction to a diagnosis of cancer. In the days that follow a diagnosis people often replay the situation when the doctor told them they had cancer over and over in their minds. People can feel as though the world around them is unreal, time slows down, it can feel like being underwater almost: the world feels muffled and foggy.

In the weeks that follow many people will describe their emotions as being like a rollercoaster. Emotions will range from fear and panic, anger, and regret, sadness and loss, to times of being more relaxed and even times of feeling calm.

It is really important to say at the outset that there is no right way to feel when you have cancer. There is no right emotional response to cancer.

There are emotions that many people will feel when diagnosed with cancer but there are no neat emotional stages to work through. We human beings cope in all sorts of different ways with a cancer diagnosis.

EMOTIONS DO NOT FOLLOW NICE, NEAT STAGES

It is sometimes said that there are stages such as the 'denial' stage or the 'anger' stage and that we work through them and eventually reach a happy-ever-after land of acceptance. This is not true. This is not how emotions work. There are no neat emotional stages to follow and work through. It is far more likely that you will experience many different emotions, even over the course of one day, sometimes, in the course of one hour. Emotions are not static: they don't flow in a straight line; and emotions don't always behave how we would like them to behave.

A cancer diagnosis will usually bring with it a range of emotions like shock, fear, sadness, guilt, sadness, and anger. These emotions will vary in intensity: some days feeling less intense and other days feeling like they are up at full volume. Experiencing such a range of emotions with changing intensity is totally normal. It does not mean you are losing your mind, nor does it mean that you are in some way psychologically weak, or that you are not coping.

This rollercoaster of emotions is to be expected, especially in the first few months after a cancer diagnosis. This kind of emotional rollercoaster is generally how we humans cope with a major life crisis like cancer. When we look back on other big life events, such as the death of a parent or the serious illness of a child in the family, or in the days after a car crash – our typical emotional state is upended: it's like suddenly hitting emotional turbulence.

What is likely to happen is that with time the emotions will settle. They will become less intense and more predictable. It is generally thought that the first couple of months after a cancer diagnosis will most likely be the time of heightened emotional upset. This will of course depend on many factors such as the type of cancer and the extent of social supports available. One should expect the first two months to be emotionally unpredictable, expect to be blindsided by emotions, and know that this will settle.

TYPICAL EMOTIONS THAT COME WITH A CANCER DIAGNOSIS

The most common emotions people feel when diagnosed with cancer are shock, fear, sadness, anger, guilt, and hope. These emotions are likely to come and go: they are likely to feel more intense or louder some days, and less loud other days. It is very important to say that with time these emotions normally settle.

Shock

At the time of diagnosis often people feel numb and simply cannot believe that they have been diagnosed with cancer. You may think the doctors got it wrong; they got the scans mixed up or some other mistake. It is not unusual to be unable to take in much information and to keep asking the same questions, and at times you may not know who to trust. You may not want to talk to family or friends about the cancer at all. It may feel 'unreal', like you are watching your life on a television screen with the sound turned down. These are completely normal reactions to a cancer diagnosis.

Fear

It will be likely for you to feel jumpy, on edge and easily startled, and the normal things like eating and sleeping may well be disturbed. You may lose interest in food and find it difficult to sleep properly. People often describe feeling physically exhausted, but the mind is racing: this 'tired but wired' feeling is very common. You may feel frightened about the treatment and about whether it will work. You might be anxious about what will happen in the future; about your job, your finances, or how your children will cope.

It is totally normal, if very unpleasant, to be frightened when you get a cancer diagnosis and at various stages of treatment. We human beings do not do well with uncertainty and loss of control. Fear is a completely understandable response to a cancer diagnosis.

Sadness

Feeling sad is a completely normal response to cancer. Cancer interrupts life and takes away our much sought after sense of certainty in the world. It can temporarily take away our freedom, independence, and hope. Feeling sad is a completely natural and appropriate emotional reaction to loss. There can be sadness about the things you didn't do and the things you did that you may feel have contributed to your cancer.

When we're sad it's not unusual to have less energy, motivation, and sometimes changes in diet. We might sleep less or sleep more than usual; we might eat less or eat more than usual; and lose interest in things we once enjoyed. For most people sadness lessens over time, for other people it can feel like they get stuck in sadness and we can't get on with life. If you feel you have become stuck in sadness, are feeling sad most of the time, or for more than two weeks or so, it would be a good idea to talk with your GP.

Anger

It is not unusual to get angry with people around you. You may be angry at those you love most: this is perfectly normal. You may feel angry at the injustice or randomness of your diagnosis, and you may feel angry with those who don't have cancer. You might get angry with yourself for bringing cancer into your family situation.

It is very normal to ask 'Why me?' and to feel anger at hospital staff, your loved ones, and if you are religious to feel angry with God. People also experience a low-level irritability in the background most of the time, and a feeling that their fuse is just about to blow at any second.

Guilt

It is very common that people diagnosed and living with cancer feel guilt. Guilt is often understood as anger turned in on yourself. You may feel guilt for upsetting people you love or afraid that you are becoming a burden to them. You may also be feeling guilty that your family has to go through this with you. You may feel guilt for things you did in the past that you feel have caused your cancer.

Hope

After the initial shock at diagnosis many people will also feel a sense of hope. There is reason to be hopeful: there are many millions of people living with and beyond cancer across the world today because of the remarkable advances in cancer care that have taken place in recent times. There is reason to be hopeful.

NAMING EMOTIONS IS AN IMPORTANT WAY TO HELP MANAGE THEM

Managing emotions plays an important part in coping with cancer and can help you feel more in control of your illness. It has been said that if we don't learn to manage emotions, the emotions will manage us.

The first step in managing emotions is to recognise them. It is a really good first step to identify them by giving them a name, this can really help to put you back in the driving seat. The second step in managing emotions is to name them out loud with a trusted friend or family member, or a trusted healthcare professional. So when you are asked by someone you trust 'how are you?', try telling them how you're genuinely feeling: 'today I'm feeling a lot of fear, to be honest', for example. Another way to 'say them out loud' is to write them down. Many people report that keeping a journal is really helpful, it can help getting things out and also to look back on how far you have come. When we name emotions and say them out loud two things can happen. Firstly, emotions become a little more manageable, a little less over-whelming. Secondly, we begin to see how our emotions change with time.

At a time of crisis, like a cancer diagnosis, it is very normal to feel that the emotions you are feeling at that moment will last forever. The feelings of fear and anger, for example, at the time of diagnosis you may feel will last forever. Naming emotions and saying them out loud to a loved one helps us to register emotions and then notice that emotions change with time. The good news is that there is no emotional state that is permanent. Rainer Maria Rilke captured this when he wrote: 'Let everything happen to you, beauty and terror, no feeling is final.'

ADDING FUEL TO THE FIRE?

There is a powerful link between our thoughts and our emotions. Our thoughts are like fuel to a fire. If you imagine your emotions as being like a smouldering flame, then our thoughts are like fuel that can turn the smouldering flame into a raging fire. Our thinking will essentially fan the flames of our emotions. For example, it is like feeling guilty (an emotion), which is smouldering away in the background, and then we throw in thoughts about the past, things I did or things I didn't do: the smouldering guilt may turn into an inferno of emotion. This is not to say that thinking is bad; it is absolutely not: the thinking mind is extraordinary. However, we need to understand the difference between the type of thinking that leads to positive and appropriate action and the type of thinking that locks us in a thought-loop of rumination and worry. This unhelpful type of thinking fans the flame of difficult emotions.

One of the most important things we can do to manage our thinking, to learn how to not throw fuel on the fire, is to notice our thoughts. This takes practice though because a lot of our thoughts are unconscious, they are more like whispers, they happen below the surface of our awareness but nonetheless have a powerful impact on our mood. This is where awareness comes in – becoming more aware of our thoughts and tuning in to the back-ground music of thoughts is a very powerful way to help deal with difficult emotions.

We need to tune in to the thoughts, in the same way as with emotions: a really helpful way to help manage troubling thoughts is to say the thoughts out loud to someone you trust. This is where the wise words 'a problem shared is a problem halved' comes from. When we say something out loud we begin to take the power away from it. It sounds so simple, but by sharing the problem (the ideas and thoughts about a difficult situation); by saying something out loud to someone we trust, we begin to take the heat out of it.

When we bottle thoughts up we tend to get stuck in a through-loop going around and around in circles in our minds. These thought-loops are exhausting and are often the fuel that keeps troubling emotions going. Naming our emotions and saying our troubling thoughts out loud to someone we trust is not easy, and it will require lots of practice, and getting it wrong is part of the deal. Go gently, aim for little baby steps to begin with and expect to feel a little nervous. The really important point here is that we can build skills in these areas: these steps will help us develop our emotional intelligence. It takes repeated practice, bravery and as much tenderness as you can muster for yourself.

There is more in-depth information in the next chapter (Chapter four) on how to deal with the stress and challenging emotions that can come with cancer.

WHEN IT MIGHT BE GOOD TO ASK FOR PROFESSIONAL HELP

It is also very normal that even with the best support from family and friends, and despite getting better at sharing troubling emotions and thoughts, that there may be a time when you need to get help from outside your circle of friends and family.

There are times when emotions such as fear, worry, anger, guilt, or sadness become very hard to manage, they can begin to hurt too much and there is no break from them. Sometimes feelings like these can interfere with you getting on with your cancer treatment, or allowing yourself to enjoy the little things in life, or simply being able to get on with ordinary everyday activities.

It is important to know the difference between ordinary sadness and serious depression, and between ordinary worry and serious anxiety. It is important to know the signs of depression and anxiety so that you can get the help required to manage these feelings and get on with your cancer care and the rest of your life. As a very general 'rule of thumb' it can be helpful to think in terms of a two-week timeframe. If difficult feelings are interrupting your everyday functioning and impacting negatively with your enjoyment of life for more than a fortnight, it might be an indication that it would be a good idea to talk with a mental health professional. It is not unusual for people living with cancer to experience anxiety and depression over the course of their treatment and recovery. It is good to get to know the difference between ordinary sadness and depression, and the difference between ordinary worry and anxiety.

Chapter seven and eight will help you understand depression and anxiety and the 'red flags' to watch out for. Getting to know the red flags or the warning signs of when it might be a good idea to seek professional help is another way to put yourself back in the driving seat and feel more in control of your life. It is really important to say that both depression and anxiety are very treatable. It is good to be proactive: know that if we have had depression or anxiety in the past, we might be more vulnerable when a major life stressor like cancer happens. Given this, it could be helpful to see your GP earlier to work out a plan to support your mood at this difficult time.

If you feel you need the help from a professional like a counsellor, a psychiatrist, or a psychologist there are three places to make your enquiries. Firstly, your medical team may be able to refer you to the psycho-oncology team at the hospital you attend. Secondly, it is a good idea to check in with your GP; she or he will most likely know of reliable places to refer you. And finally, check in with charities like the Irish Cancer Society, ARC, or the Marie Keating Foundation. It is important to get a referral to a professional who is accredited and registered with a professional association and ideally has experience working with people who have cancer.

YOUR MIND HAS NOT CAUSED YOUR CANCER

The workings of your mind have not caused your cancer. Nor will your mind cure your cancer. Of course some behaviours can influence the likelihood of developing certain cancers, such as: excessive sun exposure, smoking, and our exposure to certain environments, including exposure to products containing asbestos. However, it is really important to say that the emotional or psychological workings of your mind have not caused your cancer.

We have to be very careful not to 'psychologise' cancer by, for example, linking cancer to how we express our emotions or how positive we are. It is an understandable thing to do: it is an attempt to gain some form of control over what we most fear. But when we psychologise an illness like cancer we run the serious risk of blaming the person who has been diagnosed with cancer. This is a form of 'victim blaming', essentially because it convinces you that something you have done emotionally or psychologically has caused your cancer.

BE CAUTIOUS: SOMETIMES MORE HARM THAN GOOD

There is ample evidence that counselling and psychotherapy provided by registered professionals can really help people living with cancer. There are, however, questionable forms of counselling and various other therapies that exist and are offered to people with cancer. These therapies and counselling approaches are often based on bizarre ideas and there is no research data to support their use.

They are often based on dangerous ideas such as cancer being the result of a lack of self-love or poor self-esteem, for example, or that cancer is anger turned in on oneself. These so-called therapies suggest that if you learned to express your anger, if you learn to love yourself, if you become more mindful, then you can beat your cancer. None of this is true.

There is no evidence base to any of this and to most professionals in the field these approaches are reprehensible and unethical. These approaches can exploit people at one of the most vulnerable times in their lives by peddling harmful, unsupported, psycho-babble.

Please do not be put off seeking help though, many people find counselling and psychotherapy an essential part of living with cancer. In the first instance contact the Irish Cancer Society Helpline if you would like to get information on accredited counsellors and psychotherapists.

THE CULT OF THE POSITIVE

If you have been recently diagnosed with cancer you will have probably been told several times to 'think positively' by many well-intentioned people, including some well-intentioned healthcare professionals. You may have been told that whatever you do 'stay positive' and 'keep the chin up' or various other off-the-cuff comments that amount to the same thing: keep positive. You may have wanted to scream at people telling you to 'keep positive'. Or maybe you thought; do they know something I don't? If I let myself feel sad, angry, afraid, or irritable is this going to give my cancer the upper hand?

The shelves of self-help sections in bookshops are filled with books about the benefits of positive thinking. Many of these books promise that you can heal your illness, your marriage, your bank account, by staying positive. Or that if you stay positive, have the right attitude, you will find the perfect partner, land the perfect job, or never get sick!

One of the dangers in all of this is that it can cause many people with cancer to blame themselves. The 'stay positive' message can suggest that getting cancer, or cancer getting worse is a result of their failure to be positive. The message often conveyed is one that says 'well if you'd stayed positive you wouldn't have gotten sick in the first place'. This kind of message is devoid of any scientific evidence. There is absolutely no basis to the notion that a lack of positivity is in any way connected to your cancer.

A lot of this kind of 'stay positive' in cancer care is part of what happens in wider society. In many parts of our culture we are obsessed with positivity.

One of the terrible downsides is that this obsession with 'staying positive' can be used to blame the victim.

The obsession with positivity suggests that somehow the person's weak psychological make-up, weak character or will, their lack of positivity, is why they got cancer. As a result, many people with cancer are left feeling guilty for not being positive all their lives, and wonder if their lack of positivity caused their cancer. What has happened is that positivity has become a kind of cult. In the cult of the positive you have to keep believing, you cannot question the power of positivity, and those who do are cast out in the cold. In the cult of the positive you have to be 100 per cent committed to positivity – no questions asked.

The cultural obsession with positivity and the cult of the positive that seems to have wangled its way into cancer care is a terrible and unnecessary additional burden placed on people with cancer. Being forced to wear a happy face, to smile your way through treatment, at probably one of the most terrifying times of your life, is only going to make it all the more lonely, isolating, and likely to actually cause psychological distress. The cult of the positive is very influential and, like any other cult, it does not require evidence or peer-reviewed research to make up the rules.

The negative psychological impact of the cult of the positive is that the natural fear, anxiety, low mood that is a totally natural part of having cancer gets silenced. And when we are silenced we can't get the help that we need to treat the very normal and very treatable responses – like anxiety, fatigue, and depression – that often come along with cancer.

It is important to say that if by nature you are inclined to be more positive in your attitude, if you are more optimistic by nature, a 'glass half-full' person, then this is absolutely fine. If, on the other hand, you are less optimistic by nature, more a 'glass half-empty' type, that is equally fine. Being positive and optimistic is not the gold standard. Forced positivity tends to make people lonely and isolates them from the people in their lives. There are very few human beings facing cancer who will do that in a state of permanent positivity – this should not be expected. It is expected that times of positivity will be peppered with times of sadness and feeling wobbly emotionally.

THE 'BATTLE' & 'FIGHT' AGAINST CANCER

Having just looked at the potential downsides to excessive positivity now we turn to how we relate to cancer. When thinking about how we relate to cancer, it must be strongly emphasised that the language we use to describe cancer, the words we use, really matter. We hear that such a person has 'put up a great battle against cancer', or that they 'lost the battle', or about the 'fight against cancer' she or he mounted. Sometimes this language refers to the demanding rounds of chemotherapy, surgeries, and radiotherapy many people have to go through, and for some people it can be language that helps to motivate and help them feel in control. However, for many the language like 'battle' and 'fighting' is unhelpful and it can be more of a burden on people with cancer. The war-like images conveyed through words like 'battle' and 'fighting' can be a cause of additional stress, and for many the language will only increase distress. The so-called 'fight against cancer' and other war like metaphors can cause people additional distress by causing guilt – as if they are not doing their part in the battle.

The media has a terrible tendency to say that such a person 'lost their battle against cancer': this kind of terminology is not helpful as it suggests that the person with cancer is the failure. This kind of language is not used in relation to other diseases: for example, we don't fight a heart attack, or a stroke, or cystic fibrosis, or kidney disease. 'Fighting cancer' reduces a very complex disease down to winners and losers and suggests that some responsibility for the progression of disease rests with the individual.

CONCLUSION

If I learned anything over the years working with many hundreds of people with cancer it is this: in the eye of the storm of a cancer diagnosis, it is not the time to make big changes, it's time to steady the ship. In times of crisis, it is the basics that matter most: rest, fresh air, healthy food and connecting with other people are the foundation stones of everything else. It might also be the time to reach out and ask for help to steady the ship, sometimes it's helpful to seek support outside of family and friends. The Irish Cancer Society provides a telephone support service staffed by cancer nurses, this is a really good place to begin the process of seeking outside help, if you feel it might be beneficial.

At a time of crisis like receiving a cancer diagnosis, gather those who love you close, rest as much as you can, get outdoors, move your body and eat the healthiest food you can. For the next while lower your expectations, do your imperfect best and aim for the good-enough. And remember: no feeling is final.

ADDITIONAL RESOURCES

Book:
Barbara Ehrenreich, *Smile or Die: How Positive Thinking Fooled America and the World* (London, 2010)

Website & Freephone:
The Irish Cancer Society www.cancer.ie
Freephone 1800 200 700 to speak with a cancer nurse

CHAPTER 4

Understanding stress and cancer

Paul D'Alton

You wake in the middle of the night and hear a loud noise downstairs. . .
You are waiting to cross a busy road and the child beside you suddenly steps out not seeing the car coming. . .
You're out for a stroll in the park on a Sunday afternoon and suddenly a big angry dog jumps out growling and barking at you. . .

When things like this happen, we have a stress-reaction. We take a sharp and sudden intake of breath, our bodies tense up, our hearts beat faster, our hearing becomes more sensitive and our vision sharper, we're jumpy and on edge. The stress-reaction is supposed to happen when we hear the loud noise in the middle of the night, when we see the child in danger crossing the busy road, or when we're suddenly confronted by the angry dog. The stress-reaction is a completely normal way to react when there is danger. The stress-reaction was designed to keep us safe and help us survive dangerous situations.

The stress-reaction happens automatically. Without even telling you, your body and mind are assessing what is going on around you and deciding what to do in order to keep you safe. This happens in split seconds, like when you hear the loud noise downstairs in the middle of the night or when the angry aggressive dog appears in front of you. When the stress-reaction gets switched on a whole range of hormones go racing through your body. These hormones are getting us ready to take action – to run away from the growling dog or to grab the child who might walk out in front of a car on the busy road.

The stress-reaction is also described as fight-flight-freeze. This is because the hormones released by the stress-reaction are getting us ready to fight in some situations, or take flight (run away) in others, and in some situations freeze until it's all over. These stress-reactions are a completely normal set of reactions when we are in immediate danger. When the stress-reaction gets switched on, we go into a state of high-alert.

- Our heart rate and blood pressure increase, and we tend to breathe more quickly. This is helping to move oxygen and nutrients out to the big muscle groups such as the legs and arms; getting us ready to take action.
- We get flushed in the face or become pale faced. Our hands might get clammy or become cold. This is the result of blood and hormones going to other parts of the body and getting us ready to take action.
- We are on edge, jumpy, tense and trembling as the stress hormones rush through the body.
- Our eyes dilate so we can take in more light and see better and our hearing becomes more sensitive too, so we can look out for and listen for things that might be dangerous.
- The stomach muscles tense, sometimes giving the feeling of butterflies in our stomachs. The bladder and bowel may be affected, and you might lose control of them in dangerous situations. This is because the body automatically prioritises what is needed to keep you safe. So actions like digestion, for example, are paused.
- We might not feel pain immediately, like when you are in a car accident; and sometimes it is days before you feel the pain. This happens so we can take action and feel the pain later, when we are out of imminent danger.
- And our memory is affected too: sometimes the memory of an event can be crystal clear, or in other situations the memory can be blanked out.

This stress-reaction can be triggered in an instant. The loud noise, the angry dog, the child on the busy road: suddenly we are in stress-reaction. It is like the body's alarm system is activated, bells are ringing and lights are flashing, and we are on high alert.

The stress-reaction system is buried deep in the human brain and has evolved over millions of years to keep our ancestors safe in a world where there was much more danger, with many immediate life-threatening situations. There wasn't time for detailed strategy and analysis on the savannah. Our ancestors were surrounded by danger and threats, so the stress-reaction needed to be automatic. It could get switched on in a split second. Our ancestors needed a fast-acting system that would rev-up the whole body to fight any potential threat, or when they might need to run away, or take flight in order to protect themselves and their families. The human brain evolves very slowly, and we have inherited this split-second stress-reaction.

THE BIOLOGY OF THE STRESS-REACTION

Right now your heart is pumping, you are breathing, your body is digesting your last meal. We don't have to think about this or tell the body to breathe or digest food, it happens automatically. It is controlled by the nervous system. The nervous system keeps everything going: your blood flowing, your temperature regulated, your heart beating, and your lungs breathing. The nervous system has two different parts: one called the sympathetic nervous system and the other called the parasympathetic nervous system.

The sympathetic nervous system is like an accelerator in a car: it speeds things up. The parasympathetic nervous system is like the brake in a car: it slows things down. The sympathetic nervous system – the body's accelerator – is responsible for how our bodies react to danger: it revs up the body, sends hormones around the body getting us ready to take action, switching on the stress-reaction. The parasympathetic nervous system – the brake – is responsible for slowing down and keeping things in balance: it switches off the stress-reaction system. The parasympathetic system allows us to 'rest and digest'. We need both systems to be in sync, to be working together. In essence the sympathetic systems (the accelerator) job is to keep us safe when there is danger by getting us revved up and the parasympathetic systems (the brake) job is to slow us back down. Once the danger is over, the stress-reaction switched off and our ancestors experienced periods of rest and relaxation.

STRESS-REACTION: WHEN IT'S NOT NEEDED

Unlike our ancestors, the problem for many of us in today's society is that the stress-reaction doesn't seem to get switched off. The stress-reaction might have kept our ancestors safe on the savannah or in the jungle, but it seems to be running amok for many of us now. It typically takes about 20 minutes for the body to calm down after the stress-response has been switched on. So, for example, after we hear the loud noise in the middle of the night, or we're suddenly confronted by the angry growling dog, about 20 minutes after something like this happens we should begin to calm down. Our breathing should return to normal, our heart rate returns to normal, and our bodies become less tense. However, for many of us this doesn't happen: the stress-reaction doesn't stop after the danger is gone. When there is no danger or threat we are still behaving and feeling like there is. We find ourselves living with the stress-reaction switched on most of the time: we are on-edge, jittery, jumpy, tense, with shallow breathing and heart racing. In the modern world we seem to have gotten stuck in stress-reaction. So, as people living in the twenty-first century, it seems that the stress-reaction, which was supposed to protect us, is working against us at times. It is like the body's alarm system is being activated when it's not needed: we are getting hijacked by the stress-reaction.

We were not designed to live for prolonged periods like this, with the stress-reaction permanently switched on. It is physically and emotionally exhausting. Research demonstrates that with an overactive stress-reaction, we make bad decisions, our empathy for other people drops, our relationships suffer, and our overall wellbeing and mental health decline. What tends to happen for many of us is that the stress-reaction system is half-on all the time, it's running in the background. So all too often even when you find yourself sitting by the fire, warm and safe, surrounded by family and friends, the stress-reaction is humming away in the background.

WHY DOES THIS HAPPEN?: OUR THINKING IS KEY

So, just thinking about the following situations is likely to switch the stress-response on:

- The presentation at work, in front of all my colleagues, next week
- The appointment with my doctor next week to get my scan results
- The difficult conversation I have to have with my daughter
- The balance on my credit card
- The memory of the car accident

In modern times, the stress-reaction gets switched on by thinking about things. Just thinking about the presentation I have to do next week in front of lots of colleagues, or the medical appointment to get my results to a test, or the problem I'm having with one of my kids, will trigger the stress-reaction; maybe not full-blown panic but if you tune in you might notice a tightening around your stomach or your breath getting a bit more shallow.

Also, when we think back to a scary event in the past, or a time we were frightened, the stress-reaction can get switched on. Just thinking about the car accident you had last year can switch on the stress-reaction, and it is as if it is happening right now. The stress-reaction also gets switched on when you think about your phobias. Your fear of snakes, or spiders or heights, as examples; just thinking about these could trigger a stress-reaction.

What the research has found is that our thinking is key when it comes to managing stress. It confirms that the stress-reaction gets switched on even thinking about past or upcoming non-life threatening situations. The stress-reaction gets switched on when we remember difficult or frightening events from our past, things like the car accident from six months ago. In the future it might be the public speaking event, the upcoming job interview, or that phobia of snakes or spiders or heights.

WE ARE SOCIAL BEINGS

We human beings are dependent on our social support network. From infancy, once the basics are provided for, the love and close attachment we form with our caregivers, in no small part, determines our survival. In adulthood being a valued member of a family or community is an integral part of our well-being. When our place in our tribe is threatened, when our social ties and our social standing is threatened, there may be no physical threat to our bodies, or our physical safety as such, yet our minds and bodies behave as though there is.

Events like these: the phobias, the anticipation of the presentation at work, and definitely just thinking about worrying things, are not dangerous, they are not life threatening, but our bodies behave like they are. We activate the alarm system, the stress-reaction, by just thinking about things that may concern us.

OUR THINKING IS OFTEN LIKE BACKGROUND MOOD MUSIC

The other big problem for many of us is that our thinking is like background mood music: we're not always fully conscious of it but it's playing away in the background and having an effect on us. Our thinking, just like the background music, is playing away in the background, plotting and planning, strategising, telling stories, anticipating problems. And this kind of thinking switches on the stress-reaction by creating an atmosphere of threat, because we are telling our bodies to be on alert, that there is danger.

THE VERY WORD 'CANCER' SWITCHED ON THE STRESS-REACTION

There is no way to get through cancer without being stressed. It is a given. The sudden changes to lifestyle, relationships, and work, along with the often arduous treatments will, for the vast majority of people living with cancer, be stressful. And this is totally normal; to be expected. So, stress is part of the experience of having cancer and it does not reflect on you as a human being. It is to be expected.

Even hearing the word cancer will switch on the stress-reaction for many people. The word itself is likely to trigger a whole range of physical reaction: dry mouth, tightening in your stomach, shallow breathing. This is because the word cancer is still associated with death and dying, as opposed to treatment and recovery; the latter thankfully being the reality for many diagnosed with cancer today. Cancer for some people is life-threatening but there are over 100 different types of cancer – many of which are very treatable. Alarm bells of stress-reaction, nonetheless, must be expected.

The stress-reaction will naturally peak at diagnosis, during the various stages of treatment, with various procedures, when waiting for test results. It will also be likely to be high when leaving hospital, and when treatment comes to an end. It may peak again at other times like when someone you know gets a diagnosis, with any unusual symptoms, or around the anniversary of your diagnosis. It is important to say that stress is not linear: it is much more up and down. Stress will ebb and flow and catch you off guard sometimes. Stress generally does not follow precise and predictable routes.

The information overload that often comes with cancer is often a trigger for stress. The deluge of information from healthcare professionals and well-meaning friends and family can overwhelm. The completely understandable draw to google your illness, symptoms, and latest scientific trials for hours upon hours, is likely to add to this overwhelming feeling and switch the stress-reaction on.

THE TRICKY BRAIN: IT'S NOT YOUR FAULT

The big problem is that the human brain isn't always great at recognising fact from fiction. So, the human brain can get confused by what you're thinking about, what you're imagining and what's actually happening. Just thinking about the interview or the snake for example will get the body into stress-reaction mode. Or thinking about the next scan result, or the upcoming surgery. Just in the same way as when thinking about your favourite ice cream the body is getting ready for ice cream: the salivary glands and taste buds are responding to the thought of ice cream. When it comes to stress there is one really important message: it's not your fault. It's not your fault.

The human brain, the brain reading these words, feeling these feelings, is thought to have evolved over the last 500 million years. What is inside your skull is essentially a kind of software that you have inherited. The problem is this software is not entirely up to date, it has lots of glitches. One of the serious glitches is that the brain can get confused by what you are thinking about, what you are imagining, and by what's actually happening. When this confusion between fact and fiction happens, the stress-reaction is activated when it is not needed.

IT'S NOT YOUR FAULT BUT THERE ARE THINGS YOU CAN DO

The human brain is tricky, it has lots of glitches and the stress-reaction is one of them. It's not your fault. There are, however, many things that you can do to help with the stress-reaction glitch. There are things that you can do to tip the balance of the scales so you can build up the resources to meet the demands of living with cancer.

TAKE CARE OF THE BASICS: MOVE, EAT, SLEEP, REST

When it comes to coping with the normal stress that goes along with living with cancer four of the most important things you can do to manage stress is to move, eat, sleep, and rest.

Move: Getting some exercise is essential. That might be a walk, a gentle run, a leisurely cycle. The benefits of exercise cannot be overstated. The choice will depend on your treatment and overall energy levels, and if you are unsure about what form of exercise is best for you check with your GP or seek advice from your hospital team.

Eat: Aim for three meals a day, even if they are small meals. Make sure that fruit and vegetables are a part of each of these meals. Most medical teams will have a dietician attached to their team so it might be helpful to ask your doctor for a referral.

Sleep: There are a few practical things you can do to help with sleep, like avoiding caffeine from lunchtime onward. Enjoy a coffee, tea or an alcoholic drink but watch how much you are having. Coffee and tea contain a lot of caffeine, and caffeine interferes with sleep and can cause stress. Alcohol too has its downsides: it may feel like it relaxes you, but it will interfere with your sleep and stress levels. When you do wake in the middle of the night avoid looking at the clock, avoid your phone.

Rest: At times during cancer treatment, like any other stressful time in life, your sleep will be disturbed. It might be hard to sleep, the 'tired but wired' feeling, or you might get off to sleep but wake in the early morning. One way to help with this is to shift the focus from sleep to rest. We can get fixated on the number of hours of sleep we get each night; a better way to approach it might be to focus on rest.

TAKE FIVE: THINGS THAT REDUCE STRESS AFTER THE BASICS ARE LOOKED AFTER

Get outdoors: Go green and blue: the benefits of being out in nature (green) or being beside water (blue) are significant. Being in nature or beside water is reported to reduce stress, improve overall well-being, and improve sleep.

Stay connected: Keep connected with family and friends; schedule time with them. Use technology to keep connected or enjoy the blue and the green with them.

Ask for help: Many people will say 'please let me know if I can do anything' and people appreciate being asked to help in specific ways, so think through what needs to be done and ask. For example: collecting prescriptions, grocery shopping, gardening, or collecting kids.

Keep breathing: We breathe about 22,000 times a day and there is a growing interest in how breathing can help in managing stress. There are lots of approaches but probably the most simple is just to count your breaths. Just counting one on the inbreath, two on the outbreath, three on the inbreath and so on up to a count of five, and then go back and start again at one. It's a good idea to do this at the same time every day, so maybe first thing even before getting out of bed, and then maybe say mid-afternoon before you have a cup of coffee.

MINDFULNESS AND CANCER

Many people report that meditation helps them to manage stress and cope with the challenges life throws up from time to time. It is generally recommended that we look after the basics: move, eat, sleep, rest, keep close to family and friends, watch the caffeine and alcohol intake, before rushing to learn how to meditate.

Many people find mindfulness a very good way to start meditation. Mindfulness meditation involves training the mind to be more aware of the present moment and to notice when the mind becomes caught up in thoughts about the past, or gripped by fears, or obsessed by thinking and makes endless plans for the future.

As mentioned earlier, the problem for many of us is that our thoughts are like background music, we are not always fully conscious of it but it's playing away in the background. We are busy plotting and planning, strategising, telling stories, and anticipating problems. These thoughts, let run wild, often create an atmosphere of fear and threat, that in turn switch on the stress-reaction. When we get caught up in these kinds of thought-loops it is like throwing fuel on the fire and then inadvertently switching on the stress-reaction.

This is where the skills developed through learning mindfulness meditation can be really helpful. Mindfulness meditation helps increase our awareness and this is of great importance, as with greater awareness we begin to notice when the mind has become caught up in thought-loops about the past or the future. When we notice, when we are more aware, we can take action: strategies of mindfulness give us choices and can free us from the reactive nature of the human mind. Training in mindfulness meditation helps prevent us from being constantly swept away by the current of strong thoughts and emotions. We can learn to step out of the fast-flowing river of thoughts and emotions, sit on the riverbank and even momentarily feel more in control and, thus, interrupt the stress-reaction momentum. Here is a really useful website that you might like to look at if you are interested in meditation: http://franticworld.com/free-meditations-from-mindfulness/ In addition, many local cancer support centres offer eight-week mindfulness programmes for people living with cancer. You might also like to look at the Mindfulness Teachers Association of Ireland for accredited mindfulness teachers and courses in your locality: https://mtai.ie/

CONCLUSION

Stress is a completely normal response to cancer. It is to be expected. The stress-reaction is buried deep in the human brain and, at times, it misbehaves. These brains of ours are millions of years in evolution and they have glitches: the stress-reaction is one of them. It's not your fault, but there are things that you can do to help. The most important of these is looking after the basics: move, eat, rest and sleep. In time it might be helpful to look at breathing exercises or various forms of meditation that many find beneficial in managing these glitchy brains of ours.

ADDITIONAL RESOURCES

Books:
Harry Barry, *Emotional Resilience: How to Safeguard your Mental Health* (London, 2018)
Trish Bartley, *Mindfulness: A Kindly Approach to Being with Cancer* (New Jersey, 2016)
Vidyamala Burch and Danny Penman, *Mindfulness for Health* (London, 2013)

Websites:
The Psychological Society of Ireland, Find a Psychologist www.psychologicalsociety.ie/footer/PSI-Chartered-Psychologist-Online-Directory

The Mindfulness Teachers Association of Ireland www.mtai.ie

Audio:
Oliver Burkman, *The Antidote: Happiness for People Who Can't Stand Positive Thinking* (Edinburgh, 2019) available on audible and other platforms

CHAPTER 5

Getting ready to talk with your doctor

Mary Moriarty

In the weeks and sometimes months coming up to a hospital appointment most people will experience worry. People often say they cannot think about anything else other than the upcoming appointment, and they are fearful that they will receive bad news. Many people report finding it difficult to concentrate, maybe having sleepless nights, perhaps feeling irritable and out of sorts. These are normal experiences for anybody who has received a cancer diagnosis, and for people who have been living with a diagnosis for a long time. People often say: 'the worry is always there.'

Sometimes worry can get in the way of asking important questions at the appointment with your doctor. Worry can also prevent us remembering what your doctor said, or indeed telling your doctor important pieces of information that are relevant for your care. It is not unusual for people to leave their appointment with their doctor having forgotten to ask an important question or having forgotten to tell the doctor something. This can result in more worry and anxiety, more sleeplessness, and so on.

When we have accurate information, we tend to worry less. Often when there are information gaps, we fill those gaps with the worst possible scenarios and send ourselves into a spiral of anxiety and worry. Good communication plays a very important role in helping to reduce or prevent information gaps. This in turn helps to manage some of the worry and anxiety that cancer causes.

Try to remind yourself that everyone is different, and people have different priorities, concerns, worries and questions. These concerns might change at different times during your cancer treatment and during your recovery. You may have different questions and priorities than your family or friends, and that is ok.

Learning to communicate effectively with your medical team will help to lessen your worry and will improve your overall care and well-being. The relationship between you and your team is a two-way thing, with you playing your part. A helpful way to think about the nursing, medical and wider healthcare team is that they are your partners in the management of your disease. Good communication is an essential ingredient in any consultation that you have with your doctor or nurse. In order for there to be good communication, you as the patient need to be an active participant in conversations at your appointments.

Firstly do not assume that your doctor or nurse or any healthcare professional knows what is on your mind or what questions you have. Healthcare professionals cannot read your mind, they do not necessarily know what your exact worries and concerns are, they may have some idea, but they cannot read your mind.

Your nurse or doctor can only work with what you tell them, so to make sure you get the best care, it is worth preparing for the appointment in advance. It will also be most helpful for you if you speak up for yourself and say what is on your mind. In this way you are becoming an active participant in your healthcare.

Secondly, the hospital environment can be intimidating, many people find it hard to ask questions and seek clarification on something that was said during an appointment.

'ASSUMPTIONS ARE THE ENEMY OF GOOD COMMUNICATION'

It is important that you are supported in every possible way to understand what the doctors and nurses are telling you about your disease and treatment. There are a few practical suggestions that are good to think about here. Also, do some planning well in advance of your appointment.

MEDICAL JARGON

If you are having trouble understanding the medical and technical words used by your doctors and nurses, then it is really important for you to let them know. This is nothing to be embarrassed about, many people struggle with medical terminology. It is ok to ask your nurse or doctor to explain something in plain and simple English (or your chosen language), and also to ask them to repeat what they have just said, if needed. Another way of getting information is to ask the doctor if they can draw a diagram of your disease for you, and if you wish you could take the diagram home with you.

WHEN ENGLISH IS NOT YOUR FIRST LANGUAGE

If your first language is not English, the hospital can organise an interpreter to help. You should ask in advance and tell the nurses and doctors so that other options can be planned for you.

READING AND WRITING PROBLEMS

Many people have difficulty reading and writing. Your doctor or nurse will have met many patients who have problems reading or writing. Let them know so that they can make any necessary changes to help you. Bringing a support person with you can really help with this too.

HEARING AND EYESIGHT PROBLEMS

If your eyesight or hearing is not good, please tell a member of the team. That way you can get assistance to read information leaflets and hear all the information that is important for you to hear.

THE THREE PS

Once the practical issues described above are addressed it is now time to get down to the more specific planning and preparation for the appointment. This plan will be most successful if it involves the three Ps: prepare, prioritise, and participate.

Time can move speedily during appointments. For this reason some planning and preparation will hopefully mean that you have fewer information gaps after the appointment. Furthermore, some of those worries and questions going around in your head for a long time will hopefully be eased.

Step 1: Write down all your questions

In the weeks coming up to your appointment it is a good idea to create a list where you can write your questions down as they pop into your head. Perhaps create a list in the notes section of your phone or in a notebook. When a question comes into your head, write it down. In the weeks before your appointment add any of your worries to the list. Also add any symptoms that are new, or things you feel would be important to tell the team. Do not wait to do this until the night before the appointment. Add to the list any medication questions you have or changes to your medication.

Step 2: Use a notebook

Get a notebook and use it to organise your appointments. Keep all the information you receive, including contact details of the nurses and clinics you attend. Keep your hospital number or MRN (Medical Record Number) at the front of the notebook. Keep all your appointment dates. It is best not to use post-its or a couple of different notebooks, as this can cause confusion. If you are not a notebook and pen person then use your phone, iPad or PC, but do make sure you create one file, and it is backed up. Also make sure you have access to this file for your appointment.

In the same notebook keep a list of questions that you have prepared for any appointment with the medical or nursing team. Bring this notebook to your appointments and use it to write down information your nurse or doctor gives you. If you are admitted to hospital at any point, bring the notebook with you.

The list you compiled over the weeks before your appointment will help you remember what you want to ask. It will also help you to recall any new or unexplained symptoms since your last visit or since starting new medication. Be clear and specific about any new symptoms you are experiencing. Use your own words, you do not need to use sophisticated language, your doctor or nurse will understand.

Step 3: Bring someone with you

It is usually a good plan to have someone accompany you to your medical appointments. That might be a partner, family member or close friend: someone you trust. The person you choose will help you remember what was said during the appointment. Perhaps they might write down what your doctor or nurse says to you during the appointment also, as a back up to your note taking.

Virtual appointments

Sometimes hospital appointments can be over the phone or by video link. It is recommended that you prepare in the same way by making out your list of questions in advance, using your notebook, and having someone with you who can hear what is said. Additionally, before the call finishes, clarify with the doctor or nurse what you heard them say. Then, write down any important pieces of information in your notebook.

PRIORITISE

Before the appointment

Step 1: Shorten the list. Be ready

As the date approaches – the day before is best – sit down with your list of questions, giving yourself plenty of time. Look down through your list; add anything else you feel would be important to that list. Consider getting some help from a family member or an understanding friend, then start to try and shorten or compile the list. The shortened version will be your list for the appointment. A lot needs to be discussed during the consultation, for both you and the team. With that in mind, wise use of time is a helpful strategy. The doctors and nurses have tasks to complete during the appointment and you also need to ask your list of questions and queries.

Step 2: Try to get a good night's sleep

Try to get a good night's sleep the night before your appointment. Hopefully with a restful night and clear head, you will be better able to stay alert and concentrate on the conversation. Plan out your evening in advance. If you use relaxation techniques such as going for a walk, yoga, meditation or breathing techniques, then this is a good time to use the tools that you find helpful. If you do not use relaxation techniques regularly then this is probably not a good time to start. You could consider learning some techniques at another time. Other helpful suggestions might be to have a warm bath one to two hours before bedtime and/or use distraction techniques such as listening to music, watching TV, or a movie, or reading. By planning ahead and writing down everything you want to say at the appointment, even if you are awake in the middle of the night, you can remind yourself that every-thing is on your list and, therefore, it is unlikely you will forget anything.

Step 3: On the day of the appointment

From a practical perspective, try to have something to eat and drink (if you can and as long as you have not been asked to fast for blood tests, scans, or surgery) before the hospital visit. Allow yourself plenty of time for travel. If you feel hungry or stressed due to traffic or parking difficulties, it can be really hard to concentrate and focus at the appointment. Turn off your mobile phone as soon as you check in with the clinic reception. Try not to organise other important appointments for the same day. If you have a child/children, organise a babysitter or someone to collect the children from school, just in case you get delayed at the hospital.

During the appointment

- Step 1

  At the beginning of the appointment tell the doctor or nurse that you have a list of questions. That way they can ensure there is sufficient time to answer your questions.

- Step 2

  If there is something you do not understand, ask the doctor or nurse to repeat what they have said and do not be afraid to ask for clarification or further explanation.

- Step 3

  If you can, also write down the answers to your questions or anything else that is discussed. If you have brought someone with you, they may be able to do this job for you. That way, you can concentrate on the conversation.

After the appointment

As soon as you can after the appointment, sit down and write down the information you have heard. That way you have a reference point to check back on later. Most of us forget information very quickly unless we write down what we heard. This can be helpful if your partner or family asks you questions later on that day, or in the days or weeks after the appointment.

PARTICIPATE

Good communication is a two-way thing, from your doctor to you, and from you to your doctor. For many people appointments may be anxiety provoking. Perhaps you are just not used to asking questions about your health. It can be really helpful to practice asking your questions: reading your questions out loud at home can be a good way of preparing in advance.

Very often people say that they are worried about a question being a stupid question. There really is no such thing as a stupid question when it comes to your health. If this is something you worry about then here are some suggestions for you. You might say something like: I am a bit confused; can you explain that to me again?; or could you just say that to me again?; or could you write that down for me?

SUMMARY

So, as we come to the end of this chapter, it might be helpful to re-cap

1. Try your best to always prepare for appointments in advance.
2. Write your queries or questions into a notebook.
3. Summarise the day before. Write your summarised list in your notebook.
4. Bring a supportive person with you.
5. Be practical, try to have a good night's sleep and give yourself time. Eat something and travel to the hospital.
6. Repeat what you heard the doctor or nurse say.
7. Don't be afraid to ask for plain English or whatever the chosen language.
8. Remember that the nurses and doctors can't read your mind.
9. Write down the information as soon as possible after you leave the clinic room.
10. Even if your appointment is a virtual plan, prepare and participate in the same way.

These are just some ideas that you may find helpful. The summary in the table below may also be helpful to keep at the back of your notebook for future reference or as a reminder:

Before the appointment

Make a list of all your questions & any new symptoms. Also list your current medications.
Refine or shorten the list the day before.
Try to plan so that you get a good night's sleep.
Give yourself plenty of time for the journey.
Ask a family member or friend to accompany you.
Have something to eat if you are not fasting for a blood test or scan or surgery.
Make sure your mobile phone is charged up and that you have any other equipment that you need ready to go, eg.: headphones, charger, keys, coins for parking.

During the appointment

At the beginning of the appointment tell the doctor you have a list of questions.

Ask for clarification / explanation on anything unclear.

Repeat what you heard.

Ask what happens next.

Ask who you need to contact and how to contact them.

Ask when your next appointment is.

After the appointment

Sit down outside the clinic and write down what you heard. Take a few minutes to absorb the information.

Write down names and contact details of the nurses (often called the Clinical Nurse Specialist) and doctors you met.

Write down what the plan is.

Make your next appointment (if possible).

ADDITIONAL RESOURCES

Websites:

www.cancer.org/content/dam/cancer-org/cancer-control/en/worksheets/questions-to-ask-about-my-cancer.pdf

www.hse.ie/eng/services/yourhealthservice/hcharter/safertoask2.pdf

CHAPTER SIX

Adjustment to cancer

Siobhan McHale & Caoimhe McLoughlin

WHAT IS MEANT BY ADJUSTMENT?

When an individual suspects or learns that they have cancer, their life may seem to change in an instant. For others, the life changes are more gradual. For many, once the initial shock eases, they can begin a process of change that allows them to cope with their new reality. Examples of these changes might be seeking information about their diagnosis or re-arranging their daily routine to allow them to start treatment. Others may seek help from their loved ones to support them through all the worry and uncertainty. These changes can be thought of as adjustment.

For many, the adjustment period starts before the actual diagnosis, as they begin to notice changes in their body and suspect something is wrong. On a physical level they may find they have to rest more or alter their daily tasks. On an emotional level, they may become worried or upset as they wait for test results, or even deny they have a problem. Some individuals take a practical approach and jump into 'planning mode'. The process of adjustment is often fluid over time; and how a person copes at one stage of their diagnosis may be different to how they cope at another stage.

In this way, *adjustment* could be thought of as adapting to change and the process of becoming used to something new in life. From a nature or biological perspective, adjustment is essential for us to deal with challenges that crop up in our surroundings. If we think about adjustment in this way, it can also be thought of as *adaptation*: a feature that helps a species to function better in their environment, both internal and external. And so, in the context of a diagnosis of cancer, an individual who can make changes in their internal (emotional) world and external (practical, day-to-day) world may be in a better position to adjust well. This will enable them to manage their health journey in a more adaptive and helpful way; for example, in coping with the recommended treatment plan.

SPECTRUM OF ADJUSTMENT

For some people, underlying personality traits may colour how they manage their cancer journey – this means they may cope with having cancer in a similar way to how they deal with other challenges in life. For example, if you are used to taking a practical approach to problems, you may apply this to cancer-related problems too (such as focusing on a healthier lifestyle or planning treatment days well in advance). Some might have a tendency to seek extra support in times of need and won't hesitate to continue to do this, while others may choose to battle in silence and hide their worries. Some may be prone to thinking the worst, imagining the most negative outcome possible, while others may go the other extreme and assume only the best.

While there is no absolute 'normal response' to hearing or dealing with a cancer diagnosis – and people respond in different ways – it can be helpful to think of adjustment as occurring along a continuum. This continuum ranges from adaptive (helpful) adjustment to a more problematic (potentially unhelpful) adjustment disorder. Another way to think about this is the 'stress versus distress response'; while it is entirely normal to be stressed, this stress may tip into distress, where the person may need some extra support.

'STRESS VERSUS DISTRESS' RESPONSE

The word 'stress' is often viewed negatively, but this is not necessarily true. In many situations an appropriate amount of stress is an important moti-vator, improving concentration and productivity. Stress switches on a part of our brain and nervous system called the sympathetic drive: this is

47

triggered when we are faced with change or challenge. It is likely that for many getting a cancer diagnosis may trigger this response to varying degrees.

Stress that is transient or fleeting can often serve a protective role, promoting a 'healthy adaptation'. It may nudge the individual towards seeking to understand their diagnosis, that may in turn ignite realistic planning for what lies ahead. It may stir someone into helpful activity: to prompt an individual to access supports; to encourage vigilance around attending appointments; or to engage in better lifestyle choices, such as stopping smoking.

These 'adaptive' reactions will help build resilience for the challenging healthcare journey ahead. Strong emotions such as anger, guilt, fear, and worry may also occur as part of the stress response, and are appropriate, understandable and are, in fact, to be expected.

COMMON EMOTIONAL RESPONSES IN THE ADJUSTMENT PERIOD

Guilt is a common reaction as one adjusts to the news of cancer. This may take the shape of feeling shame around selfcare or lifestyle choices, or guilt around the impact of the cancer on our loved ones. It can often be difficult not to blame oneself in these circumstances. But it is worth remembering that even if a group of individuals share the same risk factors for cancer, only some of this group will go on to develop the disease. No one 'deserves' or should be blamed for getting cancer. Developing a sense of self-compassion is a helpful way of reducing a tendency to self-blame. This is a skill that does not come naturally to many, however, it may be taught and developed – sometimes with the aid of professional support such as talking therapy.

Fear is also understandable as one adjusts to their diagnosis; and it can take different forms. For some it might be the dread of the uncertainties ahead, fear of dying, or worry about how their loved ones will cope. Some may find relief and comfort in spiritual practices or pastoral care. For many individuals fears may be soothed by getting more information about their diagnosis and what to expect from treatment, which will enable the person and their carers to feel more in control.

A major part of the adjustment process is dealing with the feeling of losing a part of oneself. The changes caused by cancer can have huge implications for an individual's sense of identity – how they relate to themselves, others, and their role in life. The diagnosis and its aftermath may influence how they see themselves as a family member, friend, or provider. Physically the cancer itself may strip an individual's energy, interfering with meaningful activities associated with a sense of worth: this could range from a simple hobby to full-time work. The cancer treatment itself may be severe, leading to hair loss or disfigurement, or necessitate surgical removal of body parts. The consequences of a breast or gynaecological cancer, for example, may impact on a woman's sense of identity as a mother and partner and woman in her own right.

There may come a sense of loss as one adjusts to the many practical changes that come with a cancer diagnosis. It may happen that the individual must isolate as part of treatment, stop working, studying, or driving. These necessary adjustments may mean that they become dependent on others or see themselves as feeble and weak. Such changes may trigger a sense of loss or grief-like state for the individual, with elements of denial, anger, sadness, and acceptance, that ebb and flow over time. These common and expected emotional responses are part and parcel of the adjustment process and will affect everyone differently. It is important to remember that there is no right or wrong way to adjust, and that your experience is unique to you. Individuals will weave in and out of these emotions at different times during their cancer journey, and, for many, some days will be better than others.

Having a range of rich emotional experience is part of what makes us human, and also encourages psychological growth. It is therefore important not to 'over-medicalise' such responses, or label painful emotions as necessarily due to sickness or mental illness. Anxiety, denial, distress, and anger are all part of the healthy processing of emotions that lead to adaptive adjustment to illness. That said, it is important not to miss more serious adjustment difficulties, where a person can get stuck in such painful emotions for a prolonged period of time, to the extent that it interferes significantly with their ability to relate to others, or care for themselves.

When demands (physical or emotional) in life are high, our ability to adapt or adjust in the normal sense becomes more fragile. For example, having a diagnosis of cancer at the same time as going through a relationship breakdown or financial worries may overwhelm our coping system. This may lead to an over-triggering of the stress response in the nervous system described above – which can lead to a 'distress' response. Distress is normal in small doses; however, if left unchecked or if it is occurring the majority of the time, it can become more serious, such that it starts to interfere substantially with day-to-day life.

IMPACT OF DISTRESS: WHY DOES IT MATTER?

Distress, affecting both mind and body, is important to recognise. Even though stress and distress is often considered 'all psychological', an over-stressed system will affect physical, body systems that are crucial for healing and repair (such as hormonal and immune systems). These systems are important in influencing response to cancer treatment – for example, the effect of chemotherapy or how quickly one recovers from surgery. Recognising and treating high levels of distress as a primary adjustment response, will help to enhance both our physical and psychological strength for the health journey ahead.

Research studies have shown that long-term untreated distress can tip into a mental illness such as depression and can worsen the outlook and outcomes in people with cancer. A distressed patient may be more likely to engage in unhealthy coping habits such as poor diet, smoking, social with-drawal, or substance misuse. On a more extreme level, the distressed patient may avoid hospital appointments due to feeling overwhelmed or become clinically anxious or depressed. If they are feeling very upset and hopeless, they may stop their potentially life-saving treatment or not attend follow-ups. A depressed or severely anxious person may become passive and helpless, feeling unable to navigate the healthcare system or feel unable to derive support from those who want to help them.

WHAT INCREASES THE RISK OF ADJUSTMENT PROBLEMS?

There are certain factors that make someone more likely to experience difficulties with adjustment. Significant challenges earlier in life, such as trauma or neglect, may influence how they will feel when faced with the further challenge of a cancer diagnosis, especially as feelings become in-creasingly overwhelming. Social inequality and disadvantage are associated with higher rates of stress and mental disorder. If someone is prone to using alcohol and drugs to cope, has financial difficulties, or is isolated, they are also more likely to experience adjustment difficulties and severe distress when diagnosed with cancer.

More than 15 per cent of the general population will experience a psychiatric illness at any one time in Ireland, and this may be re-triggered or made worse by the additional physical and psychological stress of having to deal with cancer. Aspects of the cancer itself may also increase distress, such as poorly controlled pain or if the cancer itself has a poor prognosis. In some cases mental distress may be a direct consequence of treatment, for example, anxiety or confusion as a side effect of steroid therapy or from the social isolation necessary in bone marrow transplant. Social exclusion or lack of support can also increase the risk of mental health difficulties during this time. The inevitable disruption to one's life, bound with the role change of being a patient, may further increase feelings of distress and inadequacy.

WHEN MIGHT THE ATTENTION OF A MENTAL HEALTH PROFESSIONAL BE WARRANTED?

There are certain clues that help us to tell the difference between an adaptive response and one that needs professional support. The medical terms (diagnoses) for common conditions that go above the normal expected reaction are Adjustment Disorder, Depressive Disorder and Anxiety Disorders. Adjustment Disorder is the most common psychiatric diagnosis associated with cancer, affecting 15 to 30 per cent of such patients. On the more severe end, Depressive and Anxiety Disorders can arise in about 10 to 30 per cent of patients diagnosed with cancer. The differences will be described here.

ADJUSTMENT DISORDER

A diagnosis of Adjustment Disorder will be considered if a person's level of emotional distress is significantly greater and goes on for longer than would be expected, following a stressful event, but does not meet the full criteria for a Depressive or Anxiety Disorder (see Chapter seven and eight). The symptoms vary for each individual and include low mood, anxiety, change in behaviour, emotional outbursts, or a mix of these. It can cause problems in daily life, affecting relationships and work. There is often a feeling of inability to cope or plan or continue in the present situation, and the person may be unable to carry out their daily routine. Adjustment disorder usually arises within a three-month period of adaptation to a significant life event and can persist for up to six months after the life event goes away. Of course, the nature of a cancer diagnosis means the timeline can be unpredictable and symptoms can persist for longer. The stress of having cancer can be experienced in different ways at different stages, for some at the time of diagnosis, for others when starting chemotherapy or having surgery. And for others the time of discharge following successful treatment can paradoxically be the most stressful time, to the extent that it can trigger an adjustment disorder at a time when family and friends expect the individual to be most relieved and relaxed. This can be a result of the increased fear of trying to read one's own body for any signs of danger when no longer having regular clinic review, such as trying to work out if feelings of breathlessness are due to being unfit, feeling anxious, or a sign of the cancer affecting the lungs.

DEPRESSIVE DISORDER

Feeling down or low for some days during your cancer journey is to be expected. Depression is different to this and is more likely to arise if someone has been depressed in the past. Key signs of a depressive disorder include deriving no pleasure or joy from your usual activities, low energy, and persistent low mood. These symptoms must persist for most of the day, every day for a minimum of two weeks or more. Other symptoms include excessive or disproportionate guilt, significantly reduced self-esteem, feeling very hopeless or helpless, inability to concentrate, suicidal thoughts, and appetite or sleep disturbance. In severe cases an individual may hear voices or imagine things that are not real – this is called psychosis. Psychosis is rare and requires the attention of a psychiatrist, medication, and in some cases hospitalisation.

Please also see Chapter eight in this book for a more detailed discussion of depression.

ANXIETY DISORDERS

It is common to feel anxious as one goes through the various stages of the cancer journey. For most people, their anxiety will come and go in response to what is happening at the time, but for some it may persist or become severe such as in the case of Generalised Anxiety Disorder (GAD) or Panic Disorder.

Generalised Anxiety Disorder (GAD) is characterised by feeling worried and nervous about a wide range of things, every day, for most of the day, and is usually accompanied by other physical changes such as sweating, shaking, stomach churning, headache, trouble falling asleep, or muscle tension. Panic attacks are not uncommon with this condition. A panic attack is when your body experiences a sudden onset surge of intense anxiety and fear. It can come on very quickly and for no apparent reason. A panic attack can be very frightening and distressing – the person usually feels a racing heartbeat, faintness, hot flushes, chest pain, shortness of breath or shaky limbs. Other Anxiety conditions such as Obsessive Compulsive Disorder or Phobias can recur or get worse in someone who has a history of them.

Treatment for the above conditions usually takes the form of talking therapy such as Cognitive Behavioural Therapy (CBT), other therapies or supportive counselling or medication, or a combination of these. This can be carried out in the primary care (GP) setting, community or by the mental health team in the hospital. The latter may form part of the dedicated 'Psycho-oncology' team, and such services are being developed and expanded around Ireland currently, embedded within the oncology services.

Please also see Chapter seven in this book for a more detailed discussion of anxiety.

OVERLAP WITH CANCER SYMPTOMS

Many of the symptoms of cancer, such as low appetite, weight loss, and fatigue will overlap with depression. Depression if present, however, becomes distinct due to other features, such as excessive guilt, worthlessness, hopelessness, and suicidal thoughts. Similarly with anxiety disorders – while it is normal to feel anxious and panicky at certain stages of the cancer journey, the distinct features outlined above become important in distinguishing the difference between the normal reaction and more serious one which will require extra support.

ARE THERE WAYS TO PROMOTE HEALTHY ADJUSTMENT?

There is no rulebook on how best to adjust to a life-changing cancer diagnosis. An individual will likely adjust differently at different stages of their journey – be it screening, diagnosis, treatment, remission, recovery, or recurrence. Being a survivor of cancer too carries its own adjustment implications. Every individual will have a unique adjustment response, influenced by many factors, and there is no 'right' or 'wrong' way to cope. However, there are certain things that can be considered or put in place that might make it easier to manage.

Having a realistic expectation of what lies ahead helps, as this will allow you to plan and prepare for incoming difficulty. This means talking to your healthcare provider and obtaining as much information as possible. It might be preferable to have a carer accompany you to appointments – be it family member, trusted friend, or neighbour – so that someone else can process the information along with you.

It may be also helpful to write things down during consultations and to not be afraid to ask questions for clarification. It is not advisable to spend too much time on the internet 'googling' all the potential catastrophic things that can happen. Peer support can be helpful. Talking to someone who has been through it, while keeping in mind that everyone's journey is different, may provide beneficial and practical information on what to expect from the screening, diagnostic, or treatment process. It is very important to remember that your cancer journey is unique to you – your underlying health and individual circumstances will shape your treatment plan and outlook.

Some patients find it helpful to prepare a 'wellness' plan which will nourish the body and mind, building strength for the tough challenges ahead. These strategies may include scheduling regular exercise, yoga, mindfulness, or meditation, or making lifestyle changes such as cutting down on alcohol and cigarettes or eating a healthier diet. It is worth bearing in mind that 'the perfect is the enemy of good' and putting an over-emphasis on trying to get everything precisely right all the time is not sustainable and may add to further distress and guilt.

Keeping a diary of tests and appointments might be helpful, and may assist you in anticipating those hard days where you might be more tired and want to rest, or you might be keen to do something fun and enjoyable. Catching up with friends and loved ones is important to you if you have the energy. Doing things that give you meaning and purpose in life will also enhance your sense of worth and emotional resilience.

ADDITIONAL WAYS TO HELP WITH ADJUSTMENT

There has been a lot of research looking at how best to adjust to stress and distress in the physical health setting. Two of the most well-known techniques that have evolved are known as *Problem-Focused* Coping and *Emotion-Focused* Coping. Typically, successful distress management in the context of a cancer diagnosis involves both coping strategies.

A Problem-Focused strategy examines the root cause of the problem, with an aim to reduce or remove it. An example of this in the cancer setting is treating pain with painkillers, giving medications for nausea or sleep, or providing comfort measures. If the issue is more practical in nature this can also be addressed: for example, the staff in the treatment centre may be able to arrange transport for appointments or familiarise you with the ward environment prior to your day treatment/operation if this is a concern. For some, childcare or insurance may be a worry, and there is often a feasible solution to come by. If there are work concerns, the staff in the hospital may be able to arrange a social worker to come and talk to you about your financial, leave and work entitlements. For those with physical concerns, wigs or prosthetics may soothe angst in this regard.

This Problem-Focused approach is helpful in many situations, but is unlikely to work in situations where it is beyond the person or clinician's control to address the root cause of the problem. This is particularly true in relation to many cancer-related challenges, particularly when dealing with the existential fears that arise when one's own mortality is faced. In these circumstances, Emotion-Focused coping has an important role. Emotion-Focused coping involves the soothing of unpleasant or disturbing emotional responses, such as fear or anxiety. Some individuals try and remove these unpleasant feelings in unhelpful ways, such as using substances like alcohol to numb anxiety or denying the reality of what is happening. Avoidance or denial of the situation can be quite destructive in people with cancer. Research has found that individuals with cancer who used this thought process as a coping mechanism – for example pushing away the reality of what is happening by thinking 'I try to remove it from my memory', 'I try not to talk about it', and 'I try not to think about it' – had a worse outcome than those who engaged with their illness.

Positive Emotion-Focused coping strategies aim to reduce the impact of painful feelings and improve the tolerance of distress through helpful ways. These include counselling, therapy, mindfulness, and medication, and can be thought of as adaptive techniques that promote healthy adjustment throughout the cancer journey.

Talking therapies can range from supportive counselling to more in-depth psychotherapy. Not everyone likes talking about their innermost thoughts and fears, particularly to their loved ones. Many people with cancer want to avoid upsetting those close to them. Counselling provides a safe, reflective space for people to identify, express, and process their emotions in a non-judgemental and safe environment. A counsellor may help you to see things from a different perspective. They may assist you to problem solve or give you techniques to cope with anxiety or fear, such as simple breathing or relaxation exercises. In addition to counselling there are many different types of talking therapies, also known as psychotherapies. For more specific difficulties such as anxiety or depression, a specific type of psychotherapy called Cognitive Behavioural Therapy might be indicated. This is a commonly used therapy that explores distorted or negative thinking. The aim is to help the individual view troubling situations with more clarity, and therefore enable them to respond in more beneficial and adaptive ways.

Other techniques to reduce distress include meditation, mindfulness, yoga, and exercise. These strategies might be particularly good for those who struggle to engage in talking therapies or indeed can be used as a helpful addition to these therapies. Mindfulness has been shown to be particularly beneficial in people challenged with physical health problems and is a skill that can be built through meditation practice. Mindfulness is the quality of being fully present and engaged with the moment, thought, or action — free from judgement, and aware of feelings and thoughts without getting burdened by them. The benefits of mindfulness have been shown in relation to health across many domains, and specifically in individuals with cancer. Studies have shown that regular practice improves anxiety, stress, sleep, fatigue, and overall wellbeing in this group.

In more severe cases of distress or mental illness, medication can be helpful. One of the main purposes of medication is that it can help reduce distress, lift mood, or improve sleep enough to allow a person to concentrate and engage more effectively with psychological interventions. However, it should be prescribed thoughtfully, and it is important to get the correct balance between over-diagnosing mental illness in place of a proportionate adjustment and undertreating disabling symptoms. Medication usually takes the form of an anti-depressant or anti-anxiety medication and is always used alongside the other described interventions.

CONCLUSION

To conclude, a diagnosis of cancer triggers a range of adjustment responses as part of a healthy adaptive process to challenge. This adjustment affects each individual uniquely and may change over time. These adaptations are influenced by many factors, including underlying vulnerabilities, personal struggles, baseline supports, and the unpredictable nature of the cancer process itself. It is important to remember that no matter the reaction, all adjustment responses are valid for each individual. It is worth noting too, that the inner resilience and strength of patients and carers is often highlighted in times of change and need. Individuals are often capable of recognising and managing their own distress and actively building an adaptive and helpful coping system. However, it is important to be aware that we are all susceptible to our inner resources becoming over-burdened, and more serious distress is likely to be allayed with extra support and treatment. It must be recognised that this is the first step towards improving wellbeing and should make the cancer journey that little bit easier.

ADDITIONAL RESOURCES

Website:
The International Psycho-oncology Society – Patient Resources www.ipos-society.org/patients/resources
Podcasts:
Caroline Foran Podcast 'The Anxiety Podcast'www.carolineforan.com/podcast/

CHAPTER 7

My mind just won't stop racing: Anxiety and cancer

Susan Moore

ANXIETY AND CANCER

Getting a diagnosis of cancer is one of the most stressful things we can imagine. People respond in very different ways to this news. Feeling fearful or scared about the diagnosis, treatment or prognosis are very common responses. Apprehension about medical appointments, procedures, the possibility of pain and being unable to function may cause significant anxiety. However not feeling stressed or worried or feeling that you are actually coping quite well can also be normal. Some people only start to feel stressed on completing treatment. The reality is that there is no right or wrong way to deal with a cancer diagnosis.

You may need to get some extra help when feelings of stress become overwhelming or start to interfere on a regular basis with your day-to-day life. At this point, stress may have tipped over into what is referred to as an Anxiety Disorder.

These are some signs that you many need some support:
- When anxiety becomes more constant or unrelenting and lasts most of the day and for more than two weeks.
- When anxiety stops you doing things in your day-to-day life.
- When anxiety impacts your ability to attend the hospital for appointments or with the treatment for cancer. For example, some people might feel overwhelming fear about a certain procedure which might lead them to avoiding going into appointments/treatments.
- When you find that you are spending a lot of time online seeking information about your diagnosis or treatments. It may be hard to switch off from this.
- If you find yourself checking or rechecking results or needing frequent reassurance from your oncology team.

TYPES OF ANXIETY

When stress and worries start to take over, it may mean that your symptoms have tipped over into an Anxiety Disorder. This is different to the more 'normal' experience of stress in the context of a specific situation. This stress usually resolves quickly and does not take over day-to-day life. This is different to an Anxiety Disorder where the feelings can be almost constant.

Anyone can develop an anxiety disorder however it is more likely to develop in people who have a previous history of an anxiety disorder or have people in their family with an Anxiety Disorder. It is important to note that anxiety disorders are very common affecting approximately seven per cent of all people globally (Stein et al., 2017). In people with a cancer diagnosis the prevalence of anxiety disorders increases to ten per cent (Pitman et al., 2018).

Stress is a natural response to a traumatic or difficult event. It can vary from a feeling of mild apprehension to overwhelming fear. It is a familiar sensation to most of us in situations where we feel under pressure and overloaded (like job interviews or exams!). Physically we experience our heart beating faster, we have difficulty catching our breath, and we sweat. This physical reaction in our body to stress has been described as the 'fight or flight response'. Our body's 'alarm system' is thought to have evolved from the survival instincts of our ancestors living in threatening environments.

Imagine someone living in prehistoric times faced with a lion. The changes in the body, described above, are perfect for fighting or running away from the threat.

These changes are triggered by our sympathetic nervous system releasing stress hormones such as adrenaline and cortisol. The body is ready for action. Nowadays when we feel threatened, similar physical responses are triggered. Our bodies can react like this in a variety of situations, such as narrowly avoiding being hit by a car when crossing the road or in exams or job interviews. These 'normal' feelings of stress generally pass quickly and can even be helpful. We know that our performance improves (up to a point) with physiological arousal. The surge of energy and strength can help us jump out of the way of oncoming traffic.

There are other types of threats in the twenty-first century where these changes are unhelpful. There isn't a clear predator, and much of the danger is not visible. Examples such as having money worries or relationship difficulties are common. The surge of energy and strength are not necessary to deal with these worries, and the response is therefore disproportionate. The 'fight or flight' response in such situations can lead to overwhelming anxiety or panic attacks. It may lead to us fleeing or making frantic attempts to avoid a stressful situation. All of these responses are unconscious and happen before we are even fully aware of the situation.

A third response is sometimes added to make the 'fight, flight or freeze' response. Freeze is the equivalent to an animal playing dead when faced with a predator. In humans an overwhelming threat to survival can cause us to 'freeze up'. Another term to describe this is 'dissociation' where the connection between the mind and the body is lost temporarily. People can feel cut off from what is happening around them and what they are feeling in their body. In the shorter term this can be a protective state to be in.

When people start to feel anxious about something, the 'fight or flight' response can cause an increased rate of breathing. For some people this can develop into a panic attack where breathing becomes shallow. Instead of filling the lungs with air people start to breathe into the top of their chest only, taking quick, short breaths. This hyperventilation can cause low carbon dioxide levels in the blood which leads to symptoms like chest pain, tingling, numbness, dry mouth, or light headedness. This shortness of breath can be even more anxiety provoking and lead to a vicious cycle where the intensity of the panic attack can increase. These deeply unpleasant physical sensations are accompanied by negative and scary thoughts like 'I'm losing control' or 'I'm dying'.

Jane is getting dressed one day and finds a lump under her right arm. She freezes for an instant and then feels a surge of adrenaline. Her heart is pounding, and she finds it difficult to catch her breath. In the space of a few seconds her thoughts run through every possible permutation of worst-case scenarios. The thought 'it's cancer. . . I'm going to die' is echoing in her brain. She sits on the bed. She wants to finish dressing and pretend that she didn't feel anything. She forces herself to take a breath and goes into 'practical mode'. She rings her GP and makes an appointment for that day. She arranges for a neighbour to collect her children from school. Her heart is still pounding but it is more manageable now. She visits her GP who arranges for an urgent appointment with Breast Check.

Stress can occur at any or all stages during the cancer journey. Commonly we think of stress and worry in the initial stages or during treatment. However, it can frequently occur following completion of treatment for cancer. This is very understandable as this is a vulnerable time for patients when there is often a sudden reduction in support. At this point people frequently say that they were looking forward to not being in the hospital so often. Despite this, with less clinic visits and the fear of recurrence, they can feel more isolated and have more time to reflect on their experiences, leading to increasing feelings of stress. When stress and worry become overwhelming or unrelenting it may be a sign of an Anxiety Disorder. In psychiatry, for practical purposes, we group similar symptoms into different types of anxiety disorders but often features can overlap. It is also possible to experience symptoms of anxiety that don't fit neatly into any of the categories.

GENERALISED ANXIETY DISORDER

Generalised Anxiety Disorder can be described as a constant unpleasant feeling of anxiety or apprehension. The 'fight or flight' response is activated excessively. There may be no one specific trigger for the anxiety and the focus of the worry can move from one thing to another. People around you may think that the worries are trivial – getting to appointments on time or having the house clean – but as the person who is experiencing the worries, you may find them quite incapacitating. It is often associated with insomnia and physical symptoms like muscle tension, headaches, or tummy problems.

In the days before this appointment, Jane starts feeling on edge. Her stomach is in knots all the time and she has no appetite. She finds it impossible to relax or stop thinking about the treatment. At night, she lies awake with her thoughts going around in circles. She has a mammogram and a biopsy on the day of her first appointment and within a few days has been given a diagnosis of breast cancer.

PANIC DISORDER

Panic Disorder is when someone experiences recurrent panic attacks. Panic attacks are periods of intense and overwhelming anxiety and fear with symptoms like palpitations, sweating, shaking, shortness of breath, and chest tightness. Panic Disorder can be associated with a marked avoidance of leaving the house or being in situations where you feel escape may be difficult (also known as agoraphobia). Anxiety symptoms might escalate when going into a situation where the person has previously experienced a panic attack. This is known as Anticipatory Anxiety.

> *On her way into the hospital, she starts to feel hot and sweaty. Her heart is pounding. She tries to breathe in to relax but it's too hard for her to catch her breath. A tingling sensation starts in her fingers and moves up her arms. The thought 'I'm dying . . . I'm dying' is going around in her head. Her partner pulls over the car and she has an overwhelming urge to open the door and just run away. All of this lasts for about 15 minutes but feels like so much longer. When she gets to the hospital she tells the oncology team what happened. They reassure her that her symptoms sound like a panic attack and ask her if they can refer her to the psycho-oncology team, as they feel this might be helpful for her.*

ADJUSTMENT DISORDER

More persistent anxiety symptoms may be part of an Adjustment Disorder. This is a shorter-term response to a difficult or stressful situation such as a diagnosis of cancer. The symptoms typically start within one to three months of the stressful event and should resolve within six months. An Adjustment Disorder can be divided into those presenting with predominantly depressive or predominantly anxiety symptoms.

MIXED ANXIETY AND DEPRESSION

Anxiety symptoms can coexist in people who have a diagnosis of depression. This is sometimes referred to as Mixed Anxiety and Depression, and occurs more frequently in people with a cancer diagnosis.

HEALTH ANXIETY

Health Anxiety is a term used to describe a person who is preoccupied with the thought that they have a serious illness. They may misinterpret normal bodily sensations as being part of this illness. In patients who have had treatment for cancer this may take the form of a fear of cancer recurrence. They can ruminate on recurrence of symptoms and be hypervigilant with regards to such potential symptoms. They may continue to avoid certain activities or struggle to plan for the future for fear of their cancer diagnosis returning. Again, as with all the presentations described above, a moderate degree of these feelings is very normal. However, when these worries start to intrude on your everyday life and become overwhelming, it may mean that your symptoms have moved up a level and now meet the criteria for an Anxiety Disorder.

OTHER CAUSES OF ANXIETY

Sometimes the cancer itself or the treatment you are receiving can mimic the symptoms of anxiety. We know that shortness of breath and fatigue are frequently reported in patients undergoing chemotherapy and radiotherapy. Steroids, which are often prescribed as part of cancer treatment regimens (such as dexamethasone, prednisolone, hydrocortisone), can cause agitation or 'the jitters'. Patients often describe racing thoughts and being unable to relax. This overlap between medical and anxiety symptoms may be difficult to disentangle. Discussing your symptoms with your oncology team or general practitioner will help to clarify the situation.

MANAGING ANXIETY

Anxiety is a very treatable condition. There are many types of treatments often used in combination. So now let's talk about what we can do to manage all of this.

General lifestyle changes

Anxiety is something that we can do a lot to manage ourselves. Basic things like exercise and eating well are so important. Exercise particularly helps us to breathe more deeply and regularly and relaxes muscle tension. People find yoga or tai chi, with their more specific focus on breathing and relaxation, particularly helpful.

Although alcohol in the short term can help to relieve stress, it is important to be aware that when the effects wear off you may feel more stressed. Alcohol can significantly worsen the symptoms of an Anxiety Disorder and lead to a vicious cycle where alcohol is consumed to reduce the anxiety caused by the effect of withdrawal from recent alcohol intake. The Irish recommendations for safe alcohol intake is no more than 11 standard drinks for women and 17 standard drinks for men in the course of a week with 2 to 3 alcohol free days in a week and no more than 6 drinks in one session. A standard drink is a small glass of wine, a half pint of beer or a pub measure of spirits (with a bottle of wine containing seven standard drinks).

Caffeine is another culprit that may exacerbate anxiety symptoms. Caffeine is a stimulant and in moderate amounts can help you feel more alert. The context is also important. It can be so comforting to sit down with a friend for a chat over coffee. However, in higher amounts caffeine can escalate the unpleasant feelings of restlessness and nervousness. It causes insomnia and raises your heart rate. It might be helpful to look at your daily caffeine intake (including caffeinated soft drinks or energy drinks) and consider whether these may be having a negative effect.

Education

Learning about Anxiety Disorders and how they present themselves can be reassuring. People often fear that they are 'going mad' or dying when they experience overwhelming anxiety symptoms. Understanding the basis for these physical sensations can be reassuring and even empowering, particularly when we understand that they can be altered.

Psychological help

Talking about your worries and fears can be a huge relief. A type of research study called a meta-analysis which combines the results of multiple scientific research papers has looked at the effectiveness of different treatments for people with cancer who have an Anxiety Disorder. This study has shown that individual, one-to-one, or group talking therapy can be of significant benefit. Most of the studies look at the benefits of Cognitive Behavioural Therapy (CBT) which is discussed in more detail below; however, other types of therapy such as mindfulness or acceptance-based therapy have also demonstrated good benefits.

There are lots of strategies out there that can be used to deal with panic attacks. Being able to identify the early signs of anxiety in our body and having an awareness of changes in our breathing is one of the first steps. Learning and most importantly *practicing* breathing and relaxation techniques can help us to gain control over these feelings of panic.

Examining cancer-related fears can also be of benefit. Many worries about the cancer diagnosis or treatments have a basis in reality. A diagnosis of cancer has such an impact on us both physically and emotionally. It challenges us existentially. However, any tendency towards what are called cognitive distortions (or automatic ways of thinking) will only increase the intensity of these worries. Investigating worries means looking at the evidence to support whether these are realistic or unrealistic concerns. This may require input from the oncology team.

Examples of some specific types of cognitive distortions include:

- Catastrophising:
  This is when we picture the worst-case scenario. For someone who has been diagnosed with cancer, their automatic response may be 'there's no hope for me . . . I might as well give up now'. On exploring this further the patient may remember that the oncologist told them they had a good chance of recovery with treatment.
- Dichotomous thinking:
  This type of thinking is sometimes called 'black-and-white' thinking. This happens when we categorise things into extremes. Someone may feel that if their cancer cannot be cured that there is no point in having any treatment. The reality may be that treatment will allow them to stay well for many years. Going through the evidence for and against their initial automatic thought allows reframing of the situation for the person and may allow them to feel more in control over these thoughts.
- Using 'should':
  For example: 'I should be able to cope better with this chemo treatment . . . I shouldn't burden my family'. It can sometimes be helpful to imagine your response if a friend said the same thing. We are less critical to those around us than to ourselves.

If possible realistic worries can be approached in a practical, problem-solving way, such as by breaking tasks down into smaller steps. Sometimes, for realistic concerns without a clear solution, an acceptance-based approach such as mindfulness may be helpful. Psychological therapy looking at these cognitive distortions and their effect on our feelings and behaviour is called Cognitive Behavioural Therapy (CBT). There is evidence to support its benefit in treating anxiety associated with a cancer diagnosis. Cancer-related anxiety often revolves around the future and potential threats. Mindfulness is a way of bringing the thinking and focus back to the present. Mindfulness can be part of Acceptance and Commitment Therapy (ACT), which encourages people to accept their thoughts and feelings rather than rejecting or fighting them. It must always be noted that different approaches suit different people, and it may be a case of trying a few different things to find the right fit for you.

MEDICATION TO TREAT ANXIETY

Antidepressants are often used to treat anxiety even if you don't feel depressed. Selective serotonin reuptake inhibitors (SSRIs) are the most commonly used (e.g.: fluoxetine, sertraline, escitalopram). They are started at a low dose and increased gradually to a therapeutic dose. When these medications are started they can cause an increase in physical tension or anxiety which usually only lasts for a short period of time until the medication gets to a steady level in your body. Very occasionally this lasts longer than a few days, and if this happens you should discuss it with your GP or psychiatrist. To minimise the risk of this happening, it may be helpful to start at half the minimum dose and increase up more gradually. The usual dose of an antidepressant to treat anxiety is the same or higher than might be required to treat depression. There should be some improvement evident within a few weeks, but it may take up to eight weeks for the full benefit to become apparent. If you have been on an antidepressant at a therapeutic dose for a period of time and there is no improvement, your doctor may suggest trying another type of antidepressant such as a serotonin-norepinephrine reuptake inhibitor (SNRI). Other types of antidepressants such as tricyclic antidepressants (TCAs) can sometimes be of benefit also.

Benzodiazepines are sedative medications that are sometimes used to manage acute anxiety in the short term. They provide rapid symptom relief. However, these medications have the potential to be addictive which is why they need to be used with caution. Nonetheless they can be very useful in some crisis situations. They are most beneficial when used on a once off basis, and not continuously. Other medications which can sometimes be prescribed included beta blockers (e.g.: propranolol), which help reduce the physical symptoms of anxiety like increased heart rate, sweating, or tremors. Pregabalin is another medication that can be used in generalised anxiety disorder to manage difficult to treat anxiety symptoms. Finally, if agitation is particularly severe, a low dose anti-psychotic mediation can be used.

If you are prescribed any medications it is important to take them as directed. If you experience any side effects or aren't clear what they are for or how to take them, you should talk to your pharmacist, hospital doctor or general practitioner. There are many patient-information leaflets available on all types of medications that will also help to guide you.

CONCLUSION

The optimal treatment is a combination of all of these elements. It may take trial and error with the team looking after you to find the right combination for you. The key message from all this is that anxiety can be treated and that you don't have to go through this feeling alone.

After experiencing a panic attack, Jane was referred to the psycho-oncology team. She saw a psychologist and was able to talk about her experiences the whole way through her cancer journey and not worry about showing her vulnerability, sadness, and anger, which she felt she had to conceal from family and friends. After the initial assessment which took place over 3 sessions, the psychologist suggested using a Cognitive Behavioural Therapy approach looking at her thoughts and trying to challenge the automatic assumptions that became more evident as their work progressed. She also linked in with her local cancer support centre that had been recommended to her by the oncology team. They provided complimentary therapies which allowed her to feel cared for. She also found that the practical support around her entitlements and social welfare eased some of her financial worries which had been contributing to her overall anxiety.

Over time her anxiety improved but she still felt overwhelming apprehension coming into hospital appointments. She was referred to the psychiatrist with the psycho-oncology team who prescribed an SSRI antidepressant. Jane was reluctant initially but was aware that she was having difficulty managing things generally. She started a medication called sertraline. Initially, as she had been advised, she felt nauseated. The tension in her body increased but both of these side effects settled within a week. She increased the dose gradually as prescribed. Jane didn't notice the difference herself initially but people around her commented on the fact that she seemed to be in better form. In time Jane felt like she was back to herself. She still got upset at times dealing with the treatment for cancer and side effects but felt more able to cope in general.

ADDITIONAL RESOURCES

Book:
Helen Kennerley, *Overcoming Anxiety: A Self-help Guide Using Cognitive Behavioural Techniques* 2nd edn (Sydney, 2014)

Websites:
Yourmentalhealth.ie www2.hse.ie/looking-after-your-mental-health/
Getselfhelp.co.uk www.getselfhelp.co.uk

CHAPTER 8

I've lost all interest: Depression and cancer

Tara Kingston

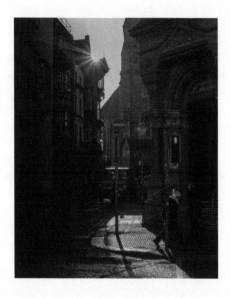

Sorcha is 51 years old and was shocked when a year ago she was told she had a diagnosis of cancer. Her mind was immediately flooded with panicky thoughts about what effect this would have on her family and her job, and that she might die of cancer, as her mother had. She felt extremely sad at times in the first week or two after diagnosis, particularly when she was on her own and had time to think, sometimes finding herself in floods of tears. It was harder than usual for her to get to sleep at night – her heart would start to race as she thought of the future while lying in bed at the end of the day. Then the following day, she would feel tired and overwhelmed, and upset by how snappy she could be with her partner and children.

Over a couple of weeks, as the initial shock wore off, things settled for her. Sorcha was busy with attending hospital appointments, going into hospital for surgery, recovering from surgery and a few months later, starting radiotherapy. Between keeping the show on the road at home and letting friends and extended family know what was going on, she hardly had time to think. Things were very tough at times – she felt extremely tired towards the end of radiotherapy, making it difficult to get things done at home, or keep up with friends or interests. And when she started on hormonal treatment and menopausal symptoms started, she felt lower and more fed up at times than was usual for her. However, good days and bad days came and went, and finally she felt she was out the far side of the challenges of the past months of diagnosis and treatment.

The doctors told Sorcha she had responded very well to treatment and that they expected her to do well. Her family were delighted that she had finished treatment and things were getting back to normal, and friends told her how well she looked. Her manager at work got in touch to see when she would like to come back. And yet, something did not feel right. She could not understand why she did not feel as happy as everyone else seemed to think she should, and this made her feel even worse. She constantly worried about the cancer coming back. Thoughts of her own mother's death from breast cancer hit her, and grief from this loss that she thought had settled, surfaced again. She waited anxiously for check-up appointments, feeling briefly relieved until the worry would start again. As the weeks went by she started to avoid family and friends as she did not seem able to chat and laugh the way she used to. She even struggled to follow the series on Netflix she loved watching as worries would crowd out her enjoyment. Sorcha started waking in the early hours of the morning with a feeling of dread in the pit of her stomach, knowing she had to struggle through another day. Even eating was no longer a pleasure, and increasingly an effort. She started to think that she had deserved her cancer, that she should have had healthier habits, and that the whole ordeal of treatment had been for nothing, given that life now did not feel worth living the way it used to.

In this story, we can see how things were very difficult for Sorcha immediately after her diagnosis, and again during treatment. But it was after treatment that she became depressed and needed extra supports for this. In this chapter we will look at what depression is, why people with cancer are at risk of depression, and what can be done about it. There will be another part of Sorcha's story towards the end of the chapter.

INTRODUCTION

Cancer can affect our mood in many different ways. However, it is rare that someone who is diagnosed with cancer will not feel down, fed-up, sad or futile at some point. What is more concerning is when those feelings become more severe, or last for longer, or have a significant impact on a person's ability to get on with their normal life. Is depression the same in cancer as in people without cancer? Well, yes and no. Yes, in that many of the symptoms are the same, and many of the same treatments are effective. No, in that there are things about cancer that make people with cancer more likely to become depressed. Also, it can be harder to diagnose depression in someone with cancer as there is often so much going on.

WHAT IS THE DIFFERENCE BETWEEN 'LOW MOOD' AND 'DEPRESSION'?

In this section, let us think about why this difference matters to health care professionals, and how they distinguish between the two. The term depression is often used in everyday language to describe low mood, but for mental health professionals or family doctors, it is used to describe something that is likely to be persistent and problematic if no help is provided. By the end of this section we hope that it may be a little clearer when it is time to take action on symptoms of depression.

Low mood can be experienced as feeling sad, worried or anxious, tired, angry, frustrated, or self-critical. These feelings are also common in depression, but one of the main differences is that low mood generally settles after a short while. By making a few changes, allowing the passage of a bit of time, or getting relief from the stress that has caused it, the unpleasant feelings associated with low mood will pass. Depression, on the other hand, is a low mood that does *not* lift with change, time or relief from a stressor. It persists day in, day out for two weeks or more, according to the definition that helps health care professionals diagnose it with more accuracy.

WHAT ARE THE SYMPTOMS OF DEPRESSION?

What, then, are the typical symptoms that are found in someone who is depressed and has cancer? The symptoms of depression are as follows:

- Low or depressed mood most days and for most of the day
- Difficulty experiencing pleasure or enjoyment in situations you normally would
- Appetite disturbance (loss of appetite or comfort eating)
- Problems with sleep (inability to get to sleep, early wakening)
- Feeling agitated or slowed down
- Being low in energy
- Feeling worthless, guilty, hopeless
- Struggling with concentration

As you might have noticed reading through the list, one of the difficulties in figuring out whether a person with cancer is depressed or not is that some of these symptoms are common in cancer patients who are *not* depressed. In particular, poor appetite, low energy levels, feeling slowed down, or struggling with concentration can also be the results of either cancer or its treatments. As a result, if someone has cancer, we pay less attention than usual to these symptoms, and more attention to depression's effects on thinking and emotion, including:

- Irritability, being short-tempered
- Tearfulness for frequent, long spells
- Lack of interest in previously enjoyed activities
- Anxiety, feeling nervous or shaky
- Feeling guilty, unworthy or deserving of punishment
- Socially isolating oneself
- Having thoughts about hurting or killing oneself

HOW COMMON IS DEPRESSION IN CANCER?

Depression occurs more commonly in certain types of cancer. It also varies depending on the phase of treatment. In general, rates of depression are higher before and during treatment, and then decrease over time (although for Sorcha, depression came after all treatment had finished). The average rate of depression is around one person in seven or eight (Niedzwiedz et al., 2019). This compares to one in 23 people in the general population (WHO, 2017). Are we surprised that the levels are three to four times higher in people with cancer than in people without? Not really. There are many things about cancer that increase someone's risk of becoming depressed, which we will look at below.

WHAT INCREASES SOMEONE WITH CANCER'S RISK OF BECOMING DEPRESSED?

There are many, many factors that have been found to play a part in making someone more likely to become depressed during their experience of cancer. The majority of these are the same factors that put someone without cancer at risk of depression: age, gender, family history of depression, level of social support and connection, history of mental health problems, social deprivation. But what, specifically, are the aspects of someone's *cancer* experience that can make it more likely for them to become depressed?

Characteristics of the cancer

People's experience of diagnosis can vary hugely from a long-awaited explanation for bothersome symptoms with a promise of successful treatment, to a devastating bolt from the blue. Having severe cancer symptoms is also a risk factor for depression: pain, nausea, fatigue, insomnia, incontinence, difficulties with sexual functioning, or loss of ability to carry out normal activities are some examples of consequences of the cancer itself and its treatment that can cause a lot of distress. The type of cancer, and its stage and grade, are other factors associated with depression. Linked to this, the prognosis and curability of the cancer can affect mood and depression. A recurrence of cancer can for some people be more of a challenge than an initial diagnosis.

Cancer treatment

Cancer treatment aims to improve the outcome for a person who has cancer. However, treatments have the potential to cause depression. For example, some treatments have a direct impact on mood (e.g., steroids, some treatments for nausea, hormonal treatments for both prostate and breast cancer, specific immunotherapy/chemotherapy agents), and therefore people taking these medications can benefit from whoever prescribes them keeping an eye on mood, as well as other side-effects. Other treatments may have longer-term complications (e.g., infertility or secondary cancers) that may affect mood after treatment has finished. Treatments that take longer, or which have more side-effects can have a more negative influence on mood. The setting of treatment (inpatient, outpatient or day-centre) can be challenging for some people. For example, some people find being an inpatient in hospital a difficult experience, whereas for others, it may be a relief to be receiving their care in that setting. The purpose of treatment can also affect someone's mood. For example, treatment of terminal cancer might have more of an impact on mood than treatment for a cancer that was caught earlier.

WHAT KINDS OF THEMES CROP UP IN DEPRESSION IN CANCER?

We have covered the nuts and bolts of the impact of cancer and its treatment on mood. But there are themes in people's experience of cancer that crop up frequently when people talk about their cancer and its negative impact on their mood.

Loss of control is often a distressing part of people's experience of diagnosis and treatment of cancer. It can feel like your body has let you down. In addition it can be frustrating that the people treating the cancer and those around us are not aware of how difficult it can be to feel bounced from place to place, person to person, treatment to treatment.

There is much uncertainty during cancer diagnosis and treatment. For some people, anger can be a source of emotional pain, resulting from feeling that it is unfair that this experience has landed upon you, while others continue their lives unaffected.

Conversely, other people suffer from guilty feelings that you are in some way responsible for inflicting this extra burden on yourself and those around you. In addition, cancer can be a particularly lonely and isolating experience. While others may try to support you, it can be difficult to stay as connected to friends and family for many reasons – a desire to protect them, not knowing what to say to people or them not knowing what to say to you, getting tired of going over the same story with people again and again.

All of these feelings are normal but can become a problem for some people. In either case, seeking help from the support services mentioned here and within other chapters is well worth considering.

CAN PEOPLE WITH CANCER FEEL SUICIDAL?

Sadly, although rarely, suicide can be an outcome in a depressed patient with cancer, as it can in any person with depression. Fleeting thoughts of life not being worth living or of suicide are not at all uncommon in people with cancer, even when everyone around you may assume your focus is on preserving your life. It is very important that if you experience persistent or overwhelming thoughts of suicide, such as thinking life is not worth living, or planning to harm or kill yourself, that you let your family and your doctor know. There are many alternatives to help you manage your suffering, and everyone without exception deserves the support and help available in this situation.

WHY TREAT DEPRESSION IN CANCER?

'Well of course you're depressed – you have cancer.' This well-meaning sentiment is common when someone with cancer is diagnosed with depression. However, it can be unhelpful in that it implies that depressive illness is insignificant compared to the cancer itself, and that it is an inevitable, unavoidable consequence of it. *Many people who have gone through the experience of depression in cancer tell us that the cancer was fine, but the depression, most emphatically, was not.* Depression significantly affects people's quality of life and their capacity to enjoy what life has to offer. In addition, it has the potential to negatively impact on someone's ability to make their best decision about treatment planning (for example because of feelings of hopelessness or anxiety about side-effects). Sometimes people are reluctant to disclose symptoms of depression, either because of the stigma associated with mental health problems, or the incorrect idea that there is no successful treatment. Whilst one person with cancer in seven or eight will also experience depression, the rest will not. Of those who do experience depression, successful treatments exist that will not only improve quality of life but may also make cancer treatment easier to endure.

WHAT TREATMENTS ARE AVAILABLE FOR DEPRESSION IN CANCER?

A range of well-tested options are available to support people with depression in cancer. There are also many untested, unproven options that may, or indeed may not, be helpful to people. Here we will only mention those that have been properly researched and shown to be effective. For many people, simple information on looking after their mental health is enough. It is important that bothersome symptoms are controlled with help from the treating team, unnecessary stresses are addressed, and healthy lifestyle measures are considered. There are online resources and books that provide useful information on taking the best possible care of yourself.

Many people find mindfulness-based strategies and relaxation helpful, although the evidence is stronger for people who are distressed, or have low mood or anxiety, rather than those with depression. There are also particular forms of talking therapy, or 'psychological therapies', that are known to improve symptoms of depression. These include Cognitive Behavioural Therapy (CBT) and Acceptance and Commitment Therapy (ACT). CBT is a brief intervention that shows people how to identify and change problematic thought patterns and behaviours that have a negative influence on physical symptoms and emotions. ACT, on the other hand, encourages people to embrace their thoughts and feelings rather than fighting them or feeling guilty about them, to help make people more psychologically flexible. It combines mindfulness skills with the practice of self-acceptance.

Medication can also play a role in the treatment of depression. Whilst milder forms of depression can respond to psychotherapy alone, it is not always enough if symptoms are more severe or last for longer than two weeks. The cornerstone medications are antidepressants. A doctor prescribing these will make a decision on which antidepressant to choose based on effectiveness, whilst minimising both side-effects and interactions with medications you may be taking already. Other medications for short-term management of symptoms, such as those that can help with sleep or anxiety symptoms, can also play a supporting role.

Your local cancer support centre or oncology team should be able to point you in the direction of accessing good quality information or treatment. Your GP is an important resource, and for more specialist care, psycho-oncology services are now available in many hospital cancer treatment centres.

WHAT BECAME OF SORCHA?

The clinical nurse specialist attached to the oncology team noticed at a routine appointment that Sorcha did not seem herself, and mentioned it to the oncology doctor who asked Sorcha how her form had been. She told the doctor that she had been really struggling for a few months with feeling guilty, down and hopeless. The oncologist contacted the psycho-oncology team at the hospital to ask them to see her. She saw a psychiatrist first, who asked the team psychologist to see her and start CBT treatment. The psychiatrist also started her on an antidepressant when her symptoms were a little slow to settle. Over the course of two months, Sorcha and her family were relieved to see her return to herself. She still thought about the cancer, but was back to being able to lose herself in the enjoyment of chats, walks and TV. Even after the psychological therapy finished, she found herself better able to catch herself slipping into ruminating about the cancer and not let the worry take hold. She stayed on the antidepressant for nine months, and then was able to stop it, having returned to work in the meanwhile. Her cancer experience now seemed like a challenge she could learn from, rather than a battle she was losing.

CONCLUSION

It is important that depression does not go undetected in people with cancer. Sadly, this can sometimes happen due to a number of factors. It can get forgotten in the confusion of potential causes of physical symptoms such as fatigue/poor appetite, it can be minimised as a normal reaction to the life stressor that cancer clearly is, or not mentioned by the person due to concerns about the stigma of mental illness or the belief that little can be done. Our hope is that this chapter may have removed some of the obstacles that prevent people from accessing the treatment that is available and that we know to be beneficial.

ADDITIONAL RESOURCES

Books:

T. Bates, *Coming through Depression: A Mindful Approach to Recovery* (2011)

J. C. Holland and S. Lewis, *The Human Side of Cancer: Living with Hope, Coping with Uncertainty* (New York, 2000)

J. Teasdale, M. Williams, and Z. Segal, *The Mindful Way Workbook: An 8-Week Program to Free Yourself from Depression and Emotional Distress* (New York/London, 2014)

CHAPTER 9

Tired all the time: Cancer-related fatigue

Sonya Collier & Anne-Marie O'Dwyer

David completed his treatment for cancer almost 18 months ago. He had expected to feel back to himself after a couple of months and could not understand why he was still feeling exhausted much of the time. His energy levels were always low and he quickly felt weak and worn out after even the smallest of jobs. He tried to beat the tiredness by taking things easy and by resting in bed or napping during the day. When that did not work he tried to ignore his fatigue and just 'get on with things'. This seemed to only make things worse. He became very frustrated and worried that he would never feel better.

WHAT IS FATIGUE?

We all know what it is like to feel fatigued. The words 'sleepy', 'exhausted', and 'worn out' are familiar to us. To experience tiredness, perhaps from a week's work, playing sport, minding children, or 'burning the candle at both ends', is a normal experience that affects us all on a regular basis. In a healthy person, fatigue can be a normal reaction to physical or psychological stress. It helps us maintain a healthy balance between rest and activity. It protects against 'over-doing things' and allows us to recover. 'Normal' fatigue or tiredness is relieved by rest, following which we typically feel ready to face the demands of our daily life once more.

WHAT IS CANCER-RELATED-FATIGUE?

'I had never felt tiredness like this before – I was wiped out'
'It doesn't matter how long I rest or sleep, the tank is always half empty'
'Even the smallest task can feel like too much effort'
'I do any work that needs to be done in the morning 'cause I know by 11am I'm going to be good for nothing'
'It's not just my body, my brain feels tired too'

Cancer-related fatigue is very different to 'normal' fatigue. It is much more severe and distressing and it is not directly related to recent activity. Under 'normal' circumstances our tiredness at the end of the day typically reflects how busy and active we have been. A night's sleep leaves us feeling refreshed and re-energised for the day ahead.

Cancer-related fatigue produces a very different experience. People with cancer-related fatigue tell us that even when they do very little in the way of activity they feel exhausted and lacking in energy, not just at the day's end but often throughout the day. This interferes with the person's ability to live life normally. A key difference between cancer-related fatigue and fatigue that is experienced before cancer is that sleep does not help to the degree that we would expect. Even after a night's sleep, people with cancer-related fatigue can describe a lasting, overwhelming feeling of exhaustion. Cancer-related fatigue affects many thousands of people in Ireland each year. Yet until recently it has been a largely neglected problem.

Scientific definition of fatigue
A personal experience of overwhelming sustained exhaustion and decreased capacity for physical and mental work that is not relieved by rest
(*Adapted from Cella et al., 1998*)

The experience of cancer-related fatigue can be different for different people. Levels of energy and fatigue can also change over the course of treatment and recovery. People who have cancer-related fatigue may have many symptoms in common. However, just as each person's reaction to cancer and its treatment is unique, so too is their experience of cancer-related fatigue. Some people who have had cancer treatment do not get fatigued at all, whilst others find their lives controlled by fatigue. For those who do experience cancer-related fatigue, the symptoms and impact on day-to-day life can vary greatly between one person and the next.

Furthermore, for each individual person, the fatigue they experience at diagnosis may be very different to that which they experience at the beginning of treatment, the final stages of treatment, or when treatment ends. At any of these times a person may experience no fatigue, mild, moderate or severe fatigue. Whether or not someone has fatigue at one time in their cancer journey is not necessarily a predictor of how the person will be affected by fatigue at a later point.

RECOGNISING CANCER-RELATED FATIGUE: WHAT ARE THE SYMPTOMS?

Cancer-related fatigue can be characterised by the way a person feels, both emotionally and physically, and by the way in which they think and act. Some of the common symptoms described by sufferers are:

Physical Feelings	Actions	Emotions	Thoughts / Thinking
Tiredness / absence of energy	Sleeping a lot more than usual	Sadness	There is nothing I can do about fatigue
Decreased endurance	Irregular sleep pattern	Shame	Cancer will return / worsen
Weakness	Reduced socialising	Irritability	Easily distracted / unable to concentrate
Breathlessness	Napping with no obvious benefit	Frustration	Self-critical – I should be able to do more
Exhaustion	Avoidance of activity	Fear	Indecisiveness
Weariness	Decreased socialising	Anxiety	I am not coping well enough
Being worn out	Decreased work / leisure	Disappointment	I must save my energy
Aches and pains	Worry	Guilt	I must sleep as much as possible
Malnourished	Poor motivation	Anger	

WHAT IS THE RELATIONSHIP BETWEEN PERSISTENT CANCER-RELATED
FATIGUE AND DEPRESSION?

It is important to be aware that many of the symptoms described above are
also common in depression and that fatigue and depression are sometimes
confused in people who have cancer. To complicate matters further, not
only is fatigue sometimes mistaken for depression (and vice versa), the two
conditions can be very closely related. Indeed for some people fatigue and
depression or low mood are a bit like the question of the chicken and the
egg. Fatigue may be a cause in the development of depression and
depression may contribute to the development of fatigue.

Depression

↕

Fatigue

Patient Story: Leah– Low mood contributes to fatigue

*Leah had managed her cancer treatment very well. She had been very focused on her
chemotherapy and radiotherapy and was positive throughout. However she found the
months following her cancer treatment more difficult to manage. She began to think a lot
about how cancer had impacted her life. She became preoccupied with questions about
why she had gotten cancer and whether or not there was something she could have done to
prevent it. She worried about how her surgery and treatment for cancer would affect her
future and whether or not her cancer would come back. She was very sad most of the time
and she admitted to her GP that she was often unable to stop crying. She noticed that her
motivation and interest in doing things had disappeared. She also noticed that her energy
levels were low and she felt tired all the time. Her tiredness made it difficult to get back to
doing things she had enjoyed before her diagnosis, which added fuel to her low mood and
disappointment in herself.*

Patient Story: Luke – Fatigue contributes to low mood

*Luke had noticed that his feelings of tiredness had steadily increased during the course of
his chemotherapy and radiotherapy. He no longer had the energy to do the things he had
previously enjoyed. He had been unable to return to work and he was spending more and
more time alone. He was frustrated by his inability to get back into his old life now that his
treatment was over. He felt that he should be able to do much more than he was doing and
his mood became very low. With his low mood came a loss of interest in things he had
previously enjoyed. He soon started to give up doing the things he could still do. After a
while even the smallest tasks seemed to take up too much energy.*

It is vital that cancer-related fatigue and depression are not confused, and that problems with depression are not ignored. The signs of clinical depression include:

- Depressed mood (or feeling down or sad) most of the day, most days
- Ongoing loss of interest or pleasure in activities you had previously enjoyed
- Significant change in your weight or appetite
- Sleep disturbance (sleeping a lot more or a lot less than usual)
- Agitation (feeling unable to sit still) or feeling 'slowed down'
- Loss of energy
- Feelings of worthlessness or excessive feelings of guilt
- Poor concentration and decision making
- Feelings of hopelessness
- Recurrent thoughts of death or suicide

Because some of these symptoms (for example changes in weight, appetite or sleep), are common in people with cancer, it can sometimes be difficult to detect depression. However, if you have several of these symptoms including low mood and/or loss of interest or pleasure in activities for two or more weeks, or if you are concerned that your symptoms may be caused by depression or persistent low mood, it is important to discuss this with your GP or cancer team.

Do not be put off seeking this help. We often hear from patients that they feel worried or stigmatised if they speak about depression. There is nothing shameful about discussing emotional or psychological difficulties with a professional. Problems with low mood or anxiety are extremely common. With appropriate help you will feel a lot better.

WHO GETS CANCER-RELATED FATIGUE AND FOR HOW LONG?

Despite being recognised as one of the most neglected and misunderstood problems associated with cancer, it is generally agreed that cancer-related fatigue is one of the most common. Studies have found that between 70 per cent and 99 per cent of chemotherapy and radiation therapy patients report fatigue. During treatment, patients hope that fatigue is temporary, and for many that is the case, with symptoms decreasing as the time goes by. However, for others, cancer-related fatigue can persist. Cancer-related fatigue can be present before diagnosis, may worsen during treatment and for some people can continue for months or even years after treatment is completed.

DOES CANCER-RELATED FATIGUE HAVE AN IMPACT ON QUALITY OF LIFE?

Cancer-related fatigue can be extremely distressing and disabling. Some would argue that it is the most troublesome of all cancer symptoms both during and after treatment. It is also reported to have a greater negative impact on a patient's daily functioning and quality of life than other cancer-related symptoms including pain, nausea and depression. Among patients experiencing cancer-related fatigue, the majority report that it interferes with their ability to work, perform everyday tasks and enjoy life. Studies have also found a link between cancer-related fatigue and increased levels of depression, low mood and anxiety. It is not uncommon for people who have cancer to report sadness, frustration and/or irritability which may attribute to their cancer-related fatigue. However, as discussed above, in the section on the relationship between persistent cancer-fatigue and depression, these findings should be read with caution.

IS CANCER-RELATED FATIGUE A PHYSICAL OR PSYCHOLOGICAL PROBLEM?

There is no doubt that cancer and its treatment can deplete energy resulting in reduced activity. However, our psychological response, both to having cancer and to this reduced energy, can cause a further drop in our energy and activity levels as the diagram below shows.

COMBINED PHYSICAL AND PSYCHOLOGICAL IMPACT ON FUNCTIONING

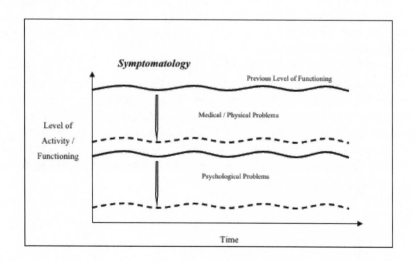

Our psychological response typically includes:

- How we *feel* – emotionally and physically about the situation
- How we *think* about the situation
- What we *do* in the situation

The story below illustrates a typical psychological response to fatigue.

Patient Story: Mary

Mary had recently completed chemotherapy and radiotherapy. She was experiencing extreme cancer-related fatigue. Her friends contacted her in Christmas week suggesting that they meet for some Christmas shopping followed by dinner. Mary regretfully declined the invitation. She later explained to her cancer nurse specialist that her energy levels would in no way permit her to walk up and down Dublin's busy Grafton Street in Christmas week. She feared that to attempt to do so would cause her to slow down her friends, cause them to be concerned about her and ruin the experience for everyone. On the day of the trip she stayed at home alone watching TV, thinking about her friends enjoying themselves, wondering why she had gotten cancer, lamenting the impact it was having on her life and worrying about what the future might hold.

In some ways Mary was right to decline a shopping trip on Christmas week. Her physical condition at that time would certainly have limited her ability to manage such an event. Indeed some might say that shopping on Grafton Street in the week before Christmas can be quite a challenge even when we are in the full of our health! However, there was no physical reason that she could not have met up with her friends for dinner after their day's shopping. Her decision not to do that was based on psychological, not physical factors – worrying about how she would look, what her friends might think about her, whether they would feel sorry for her, and feeling anxious about how she might ruin the day for them.

It can be helpful to identify and overcome situations where psychological factors, such as thoughts and feelings, are getting in the way of your activities so that you can live the best life possible despite any physical limitations. This may mean being creative about how to do things and it may also involve some compromise. In Mary's case above it could have been reducing some of her usual activities earlier in the day, getting a taxi or a lift into town, missing out on the shopping but being ready to meet her friends in the restaurant in the early evening.

WHAT CAUSES FATIGUE?

Why people experience cancer-related fatigue is not always obvious. What is clear is that it can be caused by many different factors The belief that cancer-related fatigue is due only to a small number of factors over which you have little if any control can lead to unhelpful behaviours and to feelings of helplessness, frustration and even despair. There are many factors and causes that you can tackle, whilst others once understood, can be accepted or worked around.

Cancer
Cancer itself can cause fatigue. For some people it is the first symptom that they are unwell.

Surgery
Surgery can leave people feeling tired and sore and it can take some time for energy levels to return. This is especially the case if surgery results in you being inactive for a long period of time, which can result in you becoming physically very unfit (see deconditioning below).

Chemotherapy, radiotherapy and immunotherapy
Different cancer treatments can impact energy levels in different ways. Chemotherapy, radiotherapy and immunotherapy can have a dramatic impact on your energy levels and they can play a significant role in the development of cancer-related fatigue. For people receiving chemotherapy or immunotherapy in cycles, fatigue can often follow a predictable pattern. It may get worse soon after treatment and often starts to improve in advance of the next treatment, when the cycle starts again. In the case of radiotherapy, there is often a cumulative effect with fatigue typically worsening over the course of treatment. Generally the effects of these treatments will wear off gradually over time.

Hormone therapies
Many people with cancer find that hormone therapies have a direct effect on their energy levels. They can also cause night sweats, which can lead to disrupted sleep and tiredness during the day.

Anaemia
Some people can become anaemic due to their cancer or their cancer treatment. This can lead to weakness, fatigue and breathlessness.

Pain

Pain is a common complaint among people who have cancer. This can be caused by the cancer itself, surgery or other cancer treatments. When this pain persists over time it can become very draining. It can lead to a loss of fitness (due to inactivity) and to sleep difficulties, leaving people feeling tired during the daytime.

Medications

An unwelcome side effect of some medications is fatigue.

Physical inactivity and deconditioning

Treatment for cancer can often involve long periods of inactivity either following surgery or during chemotherapy and/or radiotherapy. These are times when people can feel very physically unwell and may find themselves spending much of their time resting. While rest is an important and necessary part of recovery it can also lead to people becoming very unfit. Unused muscles become weakened and the capacity for activity in the heart and lungs decreases dramatically. This can result in a body that tires easily leaving the person huffing and puffing with aches and pains even after minimal exercise or exertion. This feeling of being 'out of shape' is also called being *deconditioned*.

Nutrition

Some people lose their appetite during treatment and find it difficult to get back into good, healthy eating habits when treatment ends. Others may deliberately limit their nutritional intake after cancer treatment due to concerns that their medication has caused or is causing them to put on weight. Others still may become very concerned about infection or food poisoning during treatment causing them to restrict their diets very significantly. For some, these food restrictions can continue even after treatment has ended and potential danger periods have passed. Extreme dieting or 'faddy' eating can mean that people are not getting enough energy from their food, contributing to feelings of fatigue. An additional problem for some people is that their cancer and/or cancer treatment may cause changes in their ability to process the nutrients necessary to provide for their energy requirements. These changes can lead to poor nutrition, resulting in fatigue.

Distress, anxiety and depression

Low mood and anxiety are not uncommon during and following cancer treatment. One of the most common symptoms of depression and low mood is a feeling of reduced energy, motivation and enthusiasm for activities. High levels of anxiety can result in poor sleep at night and persistent tension during the day causing people to feel fatigued.

Sleep disturbance

Many people experience problems with their sleep both during and after cancer treatment. Not sleeping well at night makes it more likely that you will feel very tired during the day.

Unhelpful thoughts about fatigue

The way we think about a problem can impact how we cope with that problem and ultimately whether we overcome or manage it. For example, the person who thinks two years after cancer treatment has ended that 'fatigue is the price you pay for cancer, there is nothing I can do about it', is unlikely to try to tackle their persistent cancer-related fatigue. This type of unhelpful thought is known as a self-fulfilling prophesy, whereby the belief causes one to act in a particular way that actually contributes to the belief becoming true.

Alternatively, unrealistic positive expectations can be equally problematic. The person who expects to be back to normal too quickly or who expects to be untroubled by the potential fatigue-inducing side-effects of treatments may try and do too much too soon, resulting in exhaustion and frustration that can ultimately lead the person to self-criticism and hopelessness, which in turn stops them from trying to manage their fatigue.

The domino effect and vicious cycles

As you can see from the above examples there are many causes of fatigue. Each can act alone but they can also have a 'knock-on' effect on other factors. Each connection between factors can cause fatigue to worsen. So finding ways to step in and break these links is likely to be important in managing fatigue. It is also important to remember that fatigue is a common side-effect of many cancers and their treatment. During treatment, and in the immediate weeks and months following treatment, there may be definite limits on what you can do. Acknowledging this and finding ways to manage your day around it will be important.

WHAT CAN WE DO ABOUT FATIGUE?

A first step in managing cancer-related fatigue is often just acknowledging that it is a real and valid problem that affects many (though not all) who have cancer and/or cancer treatment. In our work in St James's Hospital over the last two decades we have found that many people with cancer experienced increased distress due to the fact that they did not understand why they felt fatigued, the nature of fatigue and, in particular, why their fatigue persisted. Those who tried to ignore their fatigue during treatment, maintaining their busy lives without consideration for their reduced energy levels, and those who compared themselves unfavourably to others leading to harsh self-critical judgements, typically suffered both physically and psychologically.

The very fact that you are reading this chapter will hopefully mean that you have a better understanding of how and why fatigue can occur. Below we will discuss some things you can do to help manage it by either tackling it directly, or accepting and working around the problem.

Cancer, surgery, chemotherapy, radiotherapy and immunotherapy

Generally the effects of cancer and its treatment on energy reduce with time post treatment. Realistic expectations, helpful attitudes, taking time out, rest, prioritising activities and getting help with chores can be helpful in managing these contributing factors during, and in the weeks after, treatment. During this phase, rest, recovery and energy conservation are important. However, a growing body of evidence suggests that continuing with some gentle exercise can help protect against later fatigue. Talk to your cancer team to see if this is an appropriate option for you.

Where you experience cycles of fatigue related to your treatment weeks, it can be worthwhile planning activities that require high energy (e.g., arranging a child's birthday party) for those days when you are likely to have most energy. Where your fatigue is more constant, as is often the case during radiotherapy, try and identify time in the day when you have most energy and schedule important activities for these times.

As you move away from treatment, increasing your activity levels in a gradual manner, in small-planned steps, often works best. In this post-treatment phase, it would seem that doing too much or too little can backfire, causing you to feel more, rather than less, fatigued.

Hormone therapies, anaemia, pain and medication side effects

These are all problems that your cancer team or GP will have expertise in. They will be able to discuss your individual case with you and will be able to tell you whether a medical treatment is likely to be of help to you.

Physical inactivity and deconditioning

As mentioned previously, exercise can be helpful in preserving energy even during treatment. Talk to your cancer team to see if this is an option for you. An understanding of how inactivity affects our energy levels and the importance of gradually increasing your activity levels in the months post treatment can help. Talk to your doctor or physiotherapist about this too.

Nutrition

A balanced healthy diet can increase energy and wellbeing. Talk to the dietician on your cancer team if this is something you have concerns about.

Distress, anxiety and depression

Your cancer team or GP should be able to assess the best option for you regarding depression, anxiety or distress. They may manage your difficulties themselves or they may refer you for appropriate psychological or psychiatric treatment. This may involve psychological therapy or medication or both. Such interventions can significantly improve your mood whilst also increasing your energy levels.

Sleep disturbance

Changing some of your attitudes and behaviours around sleep can result in more restful, restorative sleep which will leave you feeling more alert and energetic during the day. There are a number of useful cognitive-behavioural therapy sleep 'apps' and self-help books that you may find useful. Alternatively, you could talk to your cancer team for a referral to the hospital psycho-oncology service. Your cancer team may be able to advise you on possible treatment options where pain, medication or hormonal treatments are at play in disrupting sleep.

CONCLUSION

In conclusion, cancer-related fatigue is a very common problem that can significantly impact quality of life. It can be experienced before, during and after treatment and is recognised as a significant problem by those living with cancer and also by some who are now cancer free. The experience of cancer-related fatigue can differ between individuals and within the same person over time. Whilst the majority of people with cancer experience some cancer-related fatigue, some people will not experience it at all, others will experience a mild loss of energy, whilst others will feel exhausted.

For some people, cancer-related fatigue will occur episodically, lasting only a few days or weeks, for others, it can last for months, or even years, after treatment is completed. Having an understanding about the many factors that contribute to cancer-related fatigue can help to reduce self-critical or self-fulfilling beliefs and lead to action to help the condition.

ADDITIONAL RESOURCES

Coping with Fatigue: Caring for People with Cancer, Irish Cancer Society Booklet (2020) www.cancer.ie/sites/default/files/2019-11/coping_with_fatigue_-_caring_for_someone_with_cancer_2017.pdf

CHAPTER 10

Living with and in a changed body

Susan O'Flanagan

Cancer and its treatment can lead to many unwelcome and often dramatic changes to the body. Cancer not only alters how the body looks, but it can also change what the body is capable of doing. Understandably, these changes to the body can be extremely difficult, or for some, impossible to accept. The changes that can happen to the body as a result of cancer are so often a source of great frustration, sadness and loss. Given this, it may be unsurprising to hear that research has shown that changes to our appearance can be one of the biggest causes of distress for people living with and beyond cancer.

Body image is about how we think, how we feel and how we behave in relation to our body and how our body works. Studies that have examined groups of cancer patients have found that about 80 per cent of people report some degree of body image concerns. Given all the visible and invisible side effects of cancer it is not surprising that body image concerns are experienced by a majority of people and are a very understandable response to the loss and change associated with living with cancer.

BODY CHANGES DUE TO CANCER

Over the course of your cancer experience your body might change in many different and difficult ways. Some of the most common changes to your body, that might be familiar to you, are things like hair loss or hair thinning, scaring, weight changes or skin changes. For some people cancer might result in permanent changes like the loss of a body part, or perhaps swelling of body parts such as the arms, which is known as lymphedema. For others it might mean living with a stoma or a feeding tube. Cancer and its treatment can also lead to a range of more functional body changes like infertility or a reduced sex drive. It can also lead to fatigue, pain, incontinence or menopausal symptoms.

For some people, the changes experienced will be quite minor, while others may experience quite significant changes or losses. Some changes will be visible to you and to others, like losing your hair. Others may be invisible such as changes to a sexual organ. It is also likely that some changes will be temporary or short term in nature, while others may be more long lasting and in some cases permanent. It is important to remember that regardless of how visible, how extensive, or how permanent these body changes are, they can still have a profound effect on how you feel about your body and yourself.

MY BODY AND I

Our body image is deeply individual. It is shaped by many varied things such as our physical appearance, our personalities, the culture we grow up in and the relationships we have. In this way, nobody comes into a cancer experience as a blank slate. We come into a cancer experience with a very long and often difficult way of thinking, feeling and behaving in relation to our bodies. Many people may have spent most of their lives being dissatisfied or even feeling shame about their shape, their size or their hairline, and that is before cancer even came into the picture.

It is important to remember that it is not how extensive the changes are that matters. What matters is your individual experience of whatever range of changes you have had to cope with. So, your experience is not only shaped by the changes the illness and treatment brings, but also by your previous relationship with your body prior to cancer.

In this way it is quite likely that people who have the same changes to their body will experience them in completely different ways. For some people minor changes may cause a great deal of distress; for others, more permanent and major changes may be accepted with ease. Some people may even view body changes in a positive light and see them as representing what the person has lived through or potentially overcome.

It is possible then that changes to the body and what it can do can be experienced in a negative, neutral or positive way. The fundamental message here is that it is not the number and type of changes you experience that is important, but it is how you experience these changes and what they mean to you.

BODY IMAGE CONCERNS ARE PAR FOR THE COURSE

Concerns about body changes are common to almost all cancer patients. So, if you are experiencing them as being difficult, you are certainly not alone. During and after treatment many people say things like 'I can't even look at my body' or 'I hate my body for letting me down'. We also know that body image concerns are not just experienced by people with a particular type of cancer, such as breast cancer. The media might lead us to believe that body image challenges are the biggest burden and problem for young or middle-aged females. This is likely because most research has focused on this group of people. However, experience tells us that body image distress can be areas of challenge and difficulty for people with all different types of cancer, for people of all ages and all sexual and gender orientations.

We know that body image is not clear cut or something that is consistently stable over our lifetime. For instance, it is likely that our body image or how we think, feel and behave towards our body might be very different at 16 compared to our experience at 50. Our body image changes over the course of our lifetime and in response to physical body changes, relationships or life events. Therefore, it is no surprise then that such a significant event as cancer will impact hugely on our body image.

Body image is also not something that can be put into clear categories, such as 'good body image' or 'bad body image'. Instead, our experience of body image concerns tends to fall on a wide continuum, from 1 (no body image concerns and generally feeling okay about your body) to 10 (very many concerns and feeling very unhappy about your body). This means that there tends to be a wide range in the experience of those living with cancer. So, some people will be completely unconcerned about the bodily changes they experience over the course of treatment. They often say things like 'I don't care what the treatment does to my body as long as it cures me'. Other people then may experience quite severe levels of body image concerns and be concerned about having treatments that will impact on how the body looks and what it can do.

You may be able to quickly identify where you are likely to fall on this continuum. But, if not, perhaps take a moment to think about the level and number of body image concerns you have at present and where you might fall on this continuum from body image dissatisfaction to body image satisfaction.

TIMING OF BODY IMAGE CONCERNS

There is no particular 'right' time to have body image concerns. In fact we know that concerns and challenges relating to body image can be present at any point over a cancer experience. Some people will be very worried about the impact of cancer and treatment on the body from the point of diagnosis. They may experience worry and upset about the thoughts or imagined images of the changes that are likely to occur. Other people may pay little or no attention to body changes until after their active treatment has finished. They may cope well with changes to their body image when the immediate changes occur, but may struggle after treatment has finished.

We also know that concerns about body image are not only experienced by people who are living with a cancer that can be cured. They can also be an issue of deep concern for people who are living with a life limiting illness or for people who are at the end of life. Our relationship with our body and what it can do is a deeply personal and important one. The significance of that relationship remains and is deserving of our kindness, attention and of support regardless of whether treatment is curative or not.

Sadly, we know that challenges with body image can be an area of distress to patients for many months and years after their initial diagnosis. However, we do also know that the level of distress or concern does tend to lessen over time. Fortunately, very many people do find ways to live even with these significant changes. Later in this chapter we will be looking at some of the coping strategies that might support you. But for now it is worth bearing in mind that for most people these difficulties tend to lessen with time, and we know that patience and kindness is essential for adapting to such significant change.

WHO IS MOST VULNERABLE?

We know that it is possible for anyone to struggle with body changes, regardless of their age, gender, sexual orientation, race or the type of cancer diagnosis they have. However, we also know that there are certain groups of people who are more likely to experience these difficulties. For example, we know from research studies that people that receive a diagnosis of breast cancer or head and neck cancer tend to struggle more with their body image.

This makes a lot of sense when we consider the visibility of the head and neck area. Or when we consider the importance of the breasts, for some women, and their connection with motherhood, femininity and sexuality. We also know about some other factors that make people more likely to experience body image difficulties. We know that females or people who are a younger age are more likely to be affected by body image concerns. Again, these are guides rather than rules and there are certainly very many older women, men, and transgender people for whom body image concerns are an area of focus and deep distress.

Research also tells us that the relationship we had with our bodies, so how we behave, think and feel about our body, prior to cancer seems to be important. It is not uncommon for people to say 'I've never accepted or liked my body'. This previous relationship can make a person more vulnerable or likely to experience body image difficulties. For example, if over your life your self-worth or how you felt about yourself was very heavily based on your appearance, you are likely to experience more difficulties if your appearance changes.

THE DOMINO EFFECT

When you experience body image difficulties as a result of disease and treatment, it is very likely that this will have a domino effect and influence a number of different aspects of your treatment and indeed your wider life. Following treatment many people describe being left 'less whole' or 'disfigured' and find it incredibly difficult to live with these changes. Again, there is a continuum or range here and some people adapt with more ease and seem to quickly embrace and make changes part of their identity. But if this is not the case for you, then you are certainly not alone.

In the next section we will explore together some of the main areas that are affected when people experience concern about body changes. It might be helpful to think about the impact of your own body changes on each of these areas.

IMPACT OF BODY CHANGES ON TREATMENT DECISIONS

When it comes to deciding on the best treatment and care plan with your medical team, it is very understandable and common for body image concerns to be on your mind. In spite of this, we know that concerns about body changes are often left out during conversations between patients and their care team. Many people describe feeling too embarrassed or too vain to bring up these worries. However, we know that it is really important and helpful to voice concerns about body changes if you have them. By voicing them it will ensure that these concerns are considered and understood by your teams when it comes to making decisions about treatment.

For some people potential changes to the body will have a big influence on the decisions we make about treatment, while for others they will be very low on the priority list. What is important is, if body changes are a concern to you, that you discuss these worries with your team. As we can see from the previous chapters, body image concerns are *very* common and remember the nurses and doctors involved in your care will have heard these concerns and questions before.

Research tells us that a significant number of people (up to 47 per cent in some studies) can experience feelings of regret about their treatment decisions. Given this, it is really important, at initial consultations and when you are planning your treatment, that you seek out clear information about the side effects of treatment. Again, it is also important to express and discuss any concerns you have about potential body changes with your healthcare team. There may be times where treatment plans can be modified or changed, and in instances where this is not possible simply being aware of your concerns will ensure your team can better support you emotionally.

THE IMPACT OF BODY CHANGES ON OUR EMOTIONS

Living in a changed body can very understandably have a big impact on how you feel and the level of distress that you experience. Being dissatisfied and self-conscious about your body changes can affect how you feel about yourself in many difficult and painful ways. People often describe body changes as being constant reminders of their illness, a reminder that they cannot escape. They may say things like 'I want to move on with my life but the changes to my appearance are a constant reminder of my cancer'. For many, this can lead to feeling different from friends and family and lead to feeling vulnerable, lonely and isolated.

Some body changes are often a difficult experience because they may make you feel less feminine or masculine. This is particularly likely if the body area affected is linked to sexuality such as the breasts for women or testes for men. If these body parts have been affected you may notice that your sense of self-worth or the confidence you once felt has changed or perhaps lessened. This is a very appropriate and understandable reaction in response to these significant losses or changes.

In general, people living with cancer can experience more worry and lower mood than the general population. This makes sense given all the demands, stresses and changes that are part of the cancer experience. We also know that how satisfied or dissatisfied we are with our bodies can also contribute to and influence our mood. For example, researchers have shown that people who have a poorer body image are more likely to experience lower mood, more worry and more stress.

Overall, it is important to remember that feelings of loss, anxiety, sadness, stress or shame, are normal feelings when you are coping with cancer and the changes it makes to your body.

THE IMPACT OF BODY CHANGES ON WHAT WE DO

Body changes that happen in response to illness and treatment tend to occur quite quickly and with very little or limited warning. This means that people often have very little time or opportunity to get their head around these changes. In light of this you might find that you are more withdrawn or you might find yourself avoiding social situations.

We know that in the early stages of the disease and treatment, this is a very normal response to these distressing and rapid changes. Many people feel that they need to take time to get used to changes themselves before facing others. For people who experience more significant difficulties with their body image, they may continue to avoid places or things they once loved over time. For example, many people might feel uncomfortable attending social events or meeting with new people after changes to their body have occurred. We know that avoiding places and activities that once offered us a sense of joy or pleasure can be an understandable but unhelpful way of coping in the longer term. If we use avoidance too often or continue to avoid things for long periods of time it can be unsupportive, and can have a negative impact on both our mood and our important relationships. Therefore, it is wise to consider how you might get this balance right. Perhaps you can start by reflecting on how your body image is impacting on what you do on a day-to-day basis.

It is very common for people to avoid looking at a specific body part post treatment. People often report 'when I have a shower and get dressed I avoid every mirror or reflective surface, I cannot face looking at myself'. Again, this is a very typical way to cope in response to significant changes to your body. Most people tend to expose themselves to affected body parts in a slow and staged way, and over time. For example, looking at a bandaged area first followed by looking at small parts of an affected area. Doing this in a paced and supportive way is most helpful.

For some people, it can prove too difficult to look at affected body parts. Just like with places or people, we know that avoiding body parts affected by cancer is not a helpful coping strategy in the long term. Support in how to face changes in a paced way is discussed later in the chapter.

THE IMPACT OF BODY CHANGES ON SEXUAL FUNCTIONING

Given the range of treatments you are exposed to as a person living with cancer, it is very understandable that they will have a knock-on effect on your intimate relationships and perhaps on your sex life. Some of the most common problems reported by both men and women are a loss of interest in sex, difficulties with orgasm, and problems with lubrication. Pain among women and erectile disorder in men are also very common.

A further, and often harrowing, side effect of illness and treatment relates to infertility among men and women. We know that challenges related to infertility can be short term or they can be longer term in nature. If you are experiencing issues with sexual difficulties or fertility then it is really important to start discussing this issue with your medical team. For some people this may seem too daunting a task. So if this is the case it might be helpful to first discuss them with a close friend, family member or even writing down your concerns to get them clear in your own mind.

Of course, for most of us discussing such personal and intimate issues is not easy. Try to keep in mind that your team is well used to and skilled in having these discussions. It is very likely that they have heard these concerns before. It may be possible to do a number of interventions to help you in the first instance and look at other support options that could be helpful. Remember that your team can only offer this support if they know you are struggling in this area: so voicing these concerns is the first step.

HOW DO I COPE WITH MY BODY IMAGE CONCERNS?

By now you will know that being unhappy with your body and what it is capable of doing is the norm rather than the exception in cancer care. So if you do find yourself struggling with concerns about your appearance and functioning then remember that you are not alone, and that you are experiencing a very normal reaction to significant loss and change. Although it may not be possible to reverse or significantly change the losses and changes that happen to your body, there are a number of effective things we can do to heal and support ourselves.

TAKE TIME TO ADJUST

First and foremost, it is important to acknowledge that learning to live with any loss or change takes time. Getting used to a changed body is no different. When we are in emotional pain it is understandable that we want someone or something to offer us a 'quick fix' or a solution to reduce our suffering. However, this is often not something that can be fixed quickly or that has a perfect solution.

Many people benefit from taking time to notice or acknowledge how they feel about their bodies. Naming or putting words on the emotional experiences we have into words, such as 'I feel angry I am in so much pain' or 'I feel less feminine since I lost my hair' can help us make more sense of the changes that have happened and the emotions that we feel. It may sound counterintuitive but we know that putting words on our feelings can help to reduce our distress. Over the course of your treatment you may need to take time to adjust a number of different times as new losses and changes emerge. During this time it can be most helpful to adopt an attitude of care, concern and kindness towards yourself rather than harsh judgement that can so quickly surface when difficult life situations arise. Allow yourself time to think about the support circle around you and to decide who in that circle you feel comfortable with and who might be open to listening to your concerns.

TALK TO YOUR HEALTHCARE TEAM ABOUT YOUR BODY IMAGE WORRIES

Although we know that the majority of people experience body image concerns, we also know that discussions about these concerns are often very rare between patients and their teams. Researchers investigating this have found that there are a number of barriers that stop these important conversations taking place. For example, many patients report feeling silly, embarrassed or guilty discussing body image concerns. They may feel that they are unimportant or less important when teams are focusing on providing lifesaving treatments.

Everyday teams are becoming more and more aware of the importance of aspects beyond a patient's physical health. Your body image is an important part of who you are and from what we illustrated above we know that it impacts greatly on many aspects of your treatment and your life. Therefore, your concern and questions about your body and the changes it is undergoing are important too.

If your medical team know about your body image concerns they can seek to support you in a variety of ways. This might include keeping these issues in mind when deciding on treatment protocols, explaining in more detail to you the rational for certain procedures.

As well as this, they might recommend medical interventions, therapies and supports that may reduce the impact of treatments on the body. It can be helpful to discuss body image early on in consultations so that your concerns can be reviewed and monitored and kept in mind as an important priority over the course of your treatment.

LOOK INTO THE PRACTICAL OPTIONS AVAILABLE TO YOU

Many people with body changes report feeling uncomfortable about their appearance particularly during social situations. Again it takes time to get used to loss and change and many people feel more comfortable with the support of various camouflage options. Depending on the type of cancer that you have and the area affected there are a number of camouflage options available to you. Some practical supports you might consider include: use of a wig or scarf for hair loss, use of a prosthesis if you have lost a body part, using camouflage make-up, wearing different types of clothing that accommodate your appearance change, or getting an artistic tattoo to cover up a scar.

Different camouflage options will be more or less relevant depending on the type of cancer you have. Remember that people tend to have very individual responses to these options and it is important to consider what feels most supportive and right for you. Your medical team or community charities are usually the best equipped places to direct you to the most relevant services available to you.

FINDING A CIRCLE OF SUPPORT YOU CAN TRUST

You might find that some people in your life just do not understand or downplay the body changes you are learning to live with. Messages from others like 'just get on with it' or 'aren't you lucky to be alive' can very unfortunately be commonplace. This type of advice is likely intended to help you move on or refocus. However, we know that it generally has the opposite effect and can feel so invalidating and dismissive of your struggle.

It might be helpful to communicate your experience and feelings to others if you find there is a mismatch between the type of support you need and the support you are receiving. For many it can be really helpful to seek support from peers or people who are also going through a cancer experience. In person and online support groups can offer you the opportunity to speak with others who have a lived experience of body changes also.

MOVING FROM FIXATION TO APPRECIATION

It makes sense that you may become more fixated or focused on appearance changes. This is particularly common in the early stages after these changes occur. Our minds are curious and they are trying to adapt and adjust to something new. It is important to allow yourself this time to get used to change. You might find that you experience a range of emotions in response to changes such as sadness, anger, surprise, disgust or curiosity. Again when adapting to change, people tend to have very different needs. For some people they might like to look at a change in the mirror for the first time on their own. Others might like a staff member or a loved one present for support. Regardless of what works best for you, we do know that it is most helpful to look at dramatic changes in a very paced and gentle way. For example, this might look like exploring a bandaged area to start and then slowly exploring part of the area without them.

It is very possible that you may be putting immense pressure on yourself to adapt or adjust to your changed body but, not everyone will come to feel comfortable with or like their changed body. Even hearing that can be helpful for some people as it can help them to stop striving or to give up the fight to achieve something that is for some unattainable. Sometimes learning to accept this reality can take the pressure off.

Changes to the body are often seen as changes to who we are and as a consequence are deeply painful. They are also changes that you likely had very little choice about. Over time, people often find that adopting a broader approach to the body can be helpful. This is where you look at the body as a whole and not just at the part you struggle most with. This might involve focusing on parts of your body that you like, or involve paying attention to what your body can do, and what you appreciate about your body now or over your lifetime.

HOW TO KNOW IF I NEED MORE HELP

Most people will experience body image changes and concern associated with these. They will feel distressed and overwhelmed as well as many other emotions, and this is normal. Over time some of your body changes may return back to normal; for others it is also likely that over time they may become less interfering or distressing.

For some people they might find that distress or overwhelm does not lessen over time and they may feel unable to cope with the challenges. For example, they may find their concern about their body is impacting their decision making about treatment, their romantic relationships or their ability to be in social situations. In these cases, going to see a therapist or counsellor may be something to consider. It may also be worth considering additional support if you have past or current difficulties that may make you more vulnerable to body image concerns. For instance, if you have had an eating disorder in the past or difficulties with sexual intimacy.

Many research studies show that seeing a psychotherapist or psychologist can lead to improved emotional wellbeing and a better relationship with your changed body. Most specialist cancer services have trained psychologists as part of their teams who will have in-depth knowledge and experience in this area. They will help you to understand your feelings more fully and come up with individual and supportive plan to help you cope with the difficulties you are having.

CONCLUSION

Our bodies, both how they look and how they function, are a deeply fundamental part of who we are. They are how we represent ourselves or show up to others and the world around us. Cancer inflicts so many changes on the body and leaves us with many visible and invisible losses. Obvious body changes can take the choice away from people about what they wish to share with the world around them. They can lead to a deep sense of distress and vulnerability. So they require tender, kind and supportive responses in each step of the journey.

ADDITIONAL RESOURCES

Written Resource:
Body Image and Cancer www.macmillan.org.uk/cancer-information-and-support/ stories-and-media/booklets/body-image-and-cancer
Managing Body Image Problems after Cancer Treatment www.hncrehab.ca/wp-content/uploads/2015/07/Managing_body_image_problems_after_cancer_treatment. pdf
Body Image and self-confidence www.cancer.ie/cancer-information-and-support/ cancer-information/cancer-treatments-and-side-effects/coping-with-side-effects/body-image-and-self-confidence

Video Resources:
Getting Your Groove Back: Sex, Reproduction and Body Image During and After Cancer

cdn.mskcc.org/playlists/getting-your-groove-back-sex-reproduction-and-body-image-
during-and-after
Cancer and Your Body Image
www.youtu.be/jz1eDe-OkQE

Podcast Resource:
Appearance Matters: The Podcast. Episode 20: Breast Cancer & Body Image.
Available on Soundcloud

CHAPTER 11

My kids . . . What do I tell them?: Talking to children about cancer

Louise O'Driscoll

For anyone receiving a diagnosis of cancer, concern for those they love is often among the first thoughts they have. This is never truer than for parents of children under 18 years of age. For this group of people with cancer every thought, every worry, may focus on the well-being of their family and how this diagnosis, treatment and prognosis will impact upon them. As parents we are hardwired to protect and nurture our children. To make sure that they survive, emotionally and physically, with the hope that they will thrive and grow into healthy, well-rounded adults. And so, a diagnosis of cancer, and with it the threat to our ability to care for and protect our children, may be uniquely distressing for parents.

When asked if children should be told about a parent having a cancer diagnosis the answer from researchers, medical social workers, psychologists and others working in the area is overwhelmingly 'yes'. The reasons for this will be talked about below. However firstly, it is important to acknowledge that this might not be what parents want to hear. It might not fit with their culture or family history, or even what they feel is right for their children.

Perhaps you have never talked about difficult feelings or emotions to your children, or even to anyone. Maybe you feel more comfortable trying to keep things as normal as possible and avoiding speaking about the change illness brings. Or you may think that you cannot or should not talk to your children about your cancer diagnosis when you do not have any certainty about what the future holds. So how do you figure out what's right for you and your family at a time when you are probably feeling physically and emotionally overwhelmed? If our main goal as parents is to protect our children, why would we even consider talking to them about cancer?

WHY TALKING HELPS

The reasons why it is recommended to include children of all ages in conversations about illness such as cancer are based on solid evidence. We know that children do not grow into resilient adults by living a life free of difficult or unpleasant experiences. We become resilient *because* of our difficult experiences, not in spite of them. It is during the more challenging times in life that we learn how to deal with difficult feelings, how to seek support, and how to trust that the people who love us will be there for us during bad times as well as good. A diagnosis of cancer within the family is a uniquely difficult experience for all involved. There is no avoiding some degree of distress. Yet within this there is an opportunity for us to support our children to learn how to talk about and manage difficult feelings, to know that we will always include and love them, and to develop their ability to empathise and care for others.

In addition, if they are left out of conversations about the illness in the family, children are likely to feel more anxious and insecure. Children, no matter how young or old, will notice changes in mood and behaviour. For example even very young children will pick up on when parents are upset without this being said, and older children will be quick to notice if conversations stop when they come into the room or if mum or dad do not go to work at the same time. In the absence of a parent giving them a way of making sense of the situation they will come up with their own stories or understandings. Often this involves a belief that something disastrous is happening. Something so bad that it cannot even be talked about. For children under 10 especially, they will be inclined to imagine that whatever is wrong, it is about them. That something they have done, said, or even thought may have caused this awful thing.

Ideally children should hear about a cancer diagnosis from a parent, guardian or another adult they trust. If the decision is made to not tell them in order to protect them, there is a chance that they will hear about the cancer from someone else or overhear a conversation. We all know how good children can be at hearing things even when you did not think they are listening! Likewise school friends may be a source of misinformation, telling children what they have heard in playgrounds and classrooms. If the information comes from somewhere other than a parent or family member, children of all ages can end up thinking that they are being left out because they do not matter or are not trusted. As a result they may be less likely to share their own fears or seek comfort from you. Left alone without support or accurate information children are likely to feel more frightened, more isolated and more worried.

While you are the expert on your children, most parents find that when they share information about their illness, their children are relieved and they can move forward together. With this in mind, rather than focusing on how to shield them from the situation entirely it may be more helpful to think about what questions they are likely to have and how you can support them.

PREPARING TO TALK

In preparing to talk to children about a cancer diagnosis our primary concern is usually 'how do I get this right?'. We can put ourselves under huge pressure to make sure that the initial conversation goes as well as it possibly can. This may mean that we try to find the perfect time for such a conversation, the perfect words to say, and worry about becoming upset ourselves. All of this, on top of managing the emotional and physical side-effects of a diagnosis, can be overwhelming and push us to delay or avoid talking. Rather than focusing on 'getting things just right' it might be more helpful to think of this first chat as just the beginning of a conversation. You can, and will, talk about things again and again so there is no need to cover everything or try to be perfect.

There is lots of information available that can help to guide and support you in talking to your children and many of these resources are listed at the end of this chapter. Before deciding how and what to say it will be helpful to first take some time to think about you and your family. You might like to do this on your own or with a partner, family member or close friend, someone who knows you well and with whom you can be open.

You could ask yourself the following:

- How am I coping with this diagnosis? What is working well? Where can I get more support if I need it? Am I comfortable asking for help?
- What did I learn about how to manage tough times growing up? Did my family talk openly about things or was information kept between adults? What do I feel worked well and what do I want to apply to parenting my/our own kids?
- How do I usually talk to my/our children about difficult feelings? Do I try to keep anything sad or worrying from them? Do I feel comfortable talking about sad or upsetting things and letting them see me upset too? If not, who could help me with this?
- What about the needs of my children? Have they had any other experiences of cancer or illness? What messages might they have gotten from this? What message do I most want to communicate to them now?

By taking the time to think about these questions you will be more able to adjust the information you read in this chapter to suit the needs of your family.

For example, you might have grown up in a family where children were protected from any 'adult' conversations and topics. While you might take a more open approach in your own parenting, a diagnosis of cancer may feel like one of those subjects that you would rather not tell your children about. So when you read that talking about cancer openly is generally most helpful you might feel stuck between what you feel comfortable with as a parent and what the guidelines say. This can be hugely draining at a time when your energy is already low. After thinking about the questions above you might decide that you do want to share the diagnosis with your children, but that you will need support, maybe from a medical social worker or psychologist.

Your answers to the questions above will guide you in preparing to talk to your children. It might become clear that you first need to get some help with your own feelings about your diagnosis. The saying 'parents should put on their oxygen mask first' applies here. We can only support our children to the extent that we can care for ourselves. Sharing our own worries with loved ones or the medical team might be helpful as might the support of a counsellor or psychologist working in the area.

The following broad guidelines might also be helpful in getting ready to talk to your children:

- Siblings often share and compare information and are sensitive to being left behind, so where possible talk to all children at the same time or on the same day. Talking to everyone together will mean providing the information at a level even the youngest can understand, and you can give more details to older children at a later point.
- If you are parenting with a partner it is helpful to have both people present or if parenting alone you might include a support person such as a best friend or family member who the children know well. That way there is support for you during the conversation and the children also know they can go to another adult if they wish to ask questions that they feel might worry or upset you.
- It might be helpful to write down what points are most important to you and practice talking these through with a partner or loved one first so that you can find the words that feel right for you. The more we can talk about what is happening in our own words, the more comfortable we are likely to be sharing this with our children.
- Try to pick a time and place where you will not be rushed and your children are well rested and free of other commitments. Try not to begin the conversation when you are tired, pressed for time, or feeling especially ill.
- While sooner is generally better in terms of starting the conversation, it may be wise for you to wait until you feel your own shock is settling or until there is some medical clarity before talking to your children.
- You might like to prepare for questions that your children might ask. In doing this, remember is it absolutely ok to say 'I do not know' or that you will find out. It is important to then come back to your child when you know more.

WHAT CHILDREN NEED TO KNOW

Children do best when they are provided with the basic information in words they can understand. This will of course depend on your individual child's age and abilities, so the suggestions below can be adapted to suit your child. (See also the resources list for detailed information on how to describe cancer and treatment)

Children will benefit from having key information such as:

- The name of the cancer; what body part it is in and how it will be treated. If the treatment plan is not yet decided, you might say 'the doctors are still waiting for some of the test results. When they have these they will be able to tell us what the plan is and then I will let you know'.
- Start with small amounts of information and focus on the present: what we know now and what the current plan is. Be open and honest while keeping

things simple. Again if you do not know the answer say that you will try to find out from the doctor and let them know as soon as possible.

- It is absolutely ok to let your children know that this is an upsetting time, and that you sometimes feel sad/scared etc. It is normal to have strong feelings about cancer but that does not mean that your family will not be able to handle it. Letting them know how you manage these feelings can give them ideas for what might help them to cope. For example you might say 'sometimes it helps to have a big cry or I ask for a cuddle, other times I go for a walk and I feel better'.
- Ask what your children want to know and try not to assume they will have the same questions or concerns as you. You can always give them more details later.
- Check your children's understanding of what you have said and ask what they already know about cancer. This is a chance to clear up any misunderstandings or myths e.g., that something they might have thought or done could have caused the cancer, that cancer is contagious or that everyone dies from cancer.
- Children will want to know how this is going to affect them. Let them know what treatment will mean in terms of who will drop them to school or activities or who will make dinner. If you do not yet have a clear plan about this let them know that you will keep them informed as things change.
- It can be helpful to talk about how illness might affect your mood as well as your body. For example, let your children know that there may be times when you will be tired, cranky or sad. This allows you to reassure them that while you might not have your usual patience or energy, you still love them just as much. It also sets an example for how they might feel and that it is ok to talk about it.
- Let them know that they can always come back and ask questions at any time. Older children especially may benefit from knowing they can talk to someone other than the parent who is ill so that they are not worried about upsetting the ill parent.
- Ask who they would like to tell. Perhaps they would like to tell their close friends, teacher or class, or nobody. This is a chance to explain how important it is to share the diagnosis with a few key people such as their teacher or closest friends. If you have confided in your friends let them know whom you have talked to and how it helped. This strengthens the idea that you, and they, do not have to face this alone.
- The question many parents dread most is 'are you going to die?'. This may be especially difficult if the family have already lost someone close to cancer. Try to be open and honest while leaving a feeling of hope. For example, it may be helpful to say something like 'people do sometimes die from cancer. But there are many different types of cancer and everyone responds differently. There are lots of new treatments and the doctors are going to give me some strong

medicine that they think will help'. (See the resources section below for talking to children about more advanced cancer).

- Children will also benefit from having some ideas about what they can do. Maybe they can help by doing their usual chores, or by giving you hugs or drawing a picture. It is important they know that they should still go to school and have fun with friends and during their activities. It may be helpful to repeat that some things will be different because of cancer (perhaps you are not working or will have to stay in hospital), but that other parts of life will continue.

Remember: this conversation is only the first of many. You can go back and talk again about the important things, so do not worry about covering everything in one go and instead follow your children's lead. They may show from their behaviour that they need the conversation to be kept short. *Remember: you're doing the best you can, and so are your children.* That might mean you burst into tears straight away or snap at your partner or that your children make a joke or misbehave. Everyone is just figuring this out, so as best as you can let go of expectations and forgive easily. *Remember: different children will have different needs depending on their age, developmental stage and temperament.* While it is helpful to talk to siblings together some follow up conversations can happen individually to provide for these needs. The following section will outline how children's understanding and needs change across their development.

HOW CHILDREN MIGHT REACT AND WAYS TO HELP

The information below is modelled on the 'Taking to kids about cancer' booklet produced by the Cancer Council, New South Wales, Australia.

New-borns, infants and toddlers (0–3 years)

Infants have little understanding of illness but will pick up on parents' anxiety and other feelings. They are sensitive to separation and may get upset when a parent is absent. Toddlers may react to physical changes in their parent (such as hair loss) or noticeable side effects such as vomiting.

New-borns and infants may react by wanting to breastfeed more for emotional comfort or becoming unsettled, especially if weaned suddenly. They are likely to be more fussy, cranky, colicly or clingy and you may notice changes in sleeping or eating habits. Toddlers may have more tantrums and increased negativity, such as saying no more often. There may be a return to behaviours such as thumb sucking, bedwetting or baby talk. Maintaining usual routines, across whomever is providing care, will support children of this age. Providing plenty of physical contact (hugs, holding, breast feeds) will help them to feel secure. You might get a sense of how your child is coping by watching their play and providing time for relaxation and calm (with music or massage) which will help them to regulate.

Pre-schoolers (3–5 years)

By now children have a basic understanding of illness. At this age children are by nature egocentric (they think everything is related to them). This contributes to beliefs that they may have somehow caused cancer, that they can catch it, or worries about who will look after them. Pre-schoolers may return to behaviours they had left behind such as thumb sucking or bed-wetting. They may seek comfort in special toys or blankets. You might observe new fears such as becoming afraid of the dark, monsters or animals. Problems with sleep, be it falling asleep or sleeping through the night might emerge, as could nightmares, sleep walking or talking. Pre-schoolers might appear more hyperactive or lethargic. You may notice a fear of separation especially at bedtime or going to preschool. Children of this age may act out with aggression (hitting/biting) or by saying hurtful things to the parent with a diagnosis. Often they will ask questions over and over even though the topic has been discussed many times before.

Providing simple, brief explanations about cancer is really important for this age group as is repeating the information and using dolls, stuffed animals or books to support understanding. Reading stories about worries, separation anxiety or nightmares can be helpful. Let pre-schoolers know that they have not caused, and will not catch cancer, and let them know what they can expect, e.g., by rehearsing who will collect them from pre-school and who will give them their dinner. They will benefit from hearing how they will be taken care of and knowing they are not forgotten. Providing opportunities and encouragement to have fun will help, as will having outlets for physical activity in order to use up excess energy. Listening and being alert to pre-schoolers feelings while maintaining usual discipline, and limit setting will help to provide understanding and containment.

Primary school children (5–12 years)

Over the course of this age range children's understanding of illness develops and they become able to take in more information about cancer cells and treatment. Younger children in this group may use simple cause-and-effect logic to make sense of things they do not understand, such as believing their behaviour caused the illness. Children of this age are also beginning to understand that people die and that death is permanent.

Again, changes in behaviour and emotions may be observed and children may be more irritable, worried, tearful or struggle to sleep. They may struggle to concentrate or pay attention in school or withdraw from friends and family. Returning to developmentally younger behaviours such as bedwetting may be observed. Changes may present as physical symptoms such as stomach aches or headaches, and children may refuse to go to school or display separation anxiety. Children of this age may try extra hard to be good or act out their worries with anger and hostility.

Assuring children of this age that nothing they did or thought can cause cancer is important even if they have not expressed this as a concern. Letting them know what changes might happen, in advance where possible, and who will take care of them will help them to feel included and prepared. Sharing your feelings with children in a straightforward way will help them to understand that it is normal to feel sad, angry etc. You can then talk about what helps and encourage children to continue with activities, sport, art etc. Suggest letting the school know what is happening and how talking to people can help: this will encourage them to be open about their feelings. Again, maintaining age-appropriate limits and involvement with household activities, such as chores, is important. This does not mean that you never allow for an off day but rather that you let your child know that you can see they are especially upset today, so it is ok to take a break from their chores but it is also important to pick them up again tomorrow.

Teenagers (12–18 years)

Over this period young people's thinking begins to be more adult-like. They can understand more abstract ideas and complex cause-and-effect relationships such as illness and symptoms. While their understanding may be more sophisticated, teenagers can struggle to manage the complexity of their emotional response. Their developmental task at this stage is to move away from their family unit towards their peers but cancer may interfere with this process creating an inner conflict.

As with younger cohorts some teenagers may react to a cancer diagnosis by becoming more insecure or dependent on parents while others will try to assume an adult role and want greater independence. They may prefer to confide in friends or feel easily criticised by attempts at support. Changes in mood such as depression or anxiety or behavioural changes such as becoming withdrawn or engaging in risk taking such as drinking or drug use may occur. Responses may manifest as physical symptoms such as headaches or stomach-aches as adolescents are vulnerable to hiding their true feelings. Lack of engagement with hobbies or academic work may also occur.

While teenagers may not always wish to talk about how they are doing it is important to let them know that you notice the changes and that you are here whenever they might like to talk. Acknowledge that they may wish to talk to peers or another trusted adult. Talk about the role changes in the family and be cautious about them taking on too many extra responsibilities while at the same time maintaining age-appropriate chores. Encourage teenagers to maintain activities and friendships and let them know how doing this allows you to support yourself emotionally. Maintaining limits and setting boundaries continues to be important and will provide a sense of safety and containment for teenagers during a potentially turbulent time. It may also be helpful to direct teenagers to resources and support where they can learn about cancer from reputable sources and talk to others in similar situations.

Signs of significant stress

Any of the above reactions are normal in response to a diagnosis of cancer within the family. In deciding whether your child might benefit from additional support it might be helpful to consider how long your child's behaviour or distress has been going on for, whether it appears to fluctuate, and if it is getting in the way of their usual activities on an ongoing (1–2 weeks) basis. It is to be expected that children, just like us, will have difficult moments, even good and bad days. They might not always feel like doing their usual activities or seeing friends, and this is ok. But if this becomes a regular or ongoing occurrence, if your usual attempts at providing support are not working, or your child appears very overwhelmed then you might want to get extra support.

Remember, you know your own children, and you know what types of behaviour and feelings are usual for them. So pay attention to your own instincts and if you are not sure then talk through your concerns with a loved one or professional such as a GP or member of your hospital team. Where to access support will depend on your personal circumstances and your child's particular needs. If you have significant concerns about your child's mood or behaviour you may wish to access the support of the child and adolescent mental health services, which you can do via your GP. For less worrying concerns you might consider the resources of your local cancer support centre, many of whom offer group and individual support for children of parents with cancer. The medical social worker or psychologist attached to your oncology team may also offer support and guidance in this instance. Similarly your child's teacher may be able to suggest supports within the school or community that may be helpful.

PARENTING WHILE LIVING WITH CANCER

The demands of cancer and its treatments coupled with the demands of parenting can be physically and emotionally exhausting. When feeling exhausted it is common for our thinking to become focused on what is going badly. We can become preoccupied with feelings of guilt and sadness about the impact of our diagnosis on family life.

At times like these it is so important to apply the same compassion and understanding to ourselves that we would to others in our position. Yes, not everything in the family home runs as smoothly as it did. Yes, there may be more ready meals and less home cooking. Of course it is not possible to maintain the exact same standards or fit everything into the family's schedule with the added demands of cancer and treatment. The first step towards going more gently on yourself is to make peace with the fact that you do not have the time or energy for everything.

From here you might make a list of all that needs to be done and decide which items are most important to you and your family. Some things could be made possible with the help of others so think about who you might recruit as a support. Fellow parents might pick up your children from activities, arrange playdates, or provide a weekly meal. Members of your religious, friendship or family group may likewise offer help. When someone offers to help, choose a task from your list that suits that person.

If asking for, or accepting, help feels really uncomfortable or new, it is useful to think about what accepting help will allow you to do. For example, by accepting a home-made dinner you will be able to use your energy to put the kids to bed and have some time to talk with them. By accepting a lift to the hospital you can rest during this time rather than focusing on stressors like parking and traffic. By acknowledging the struggle to accept help as well as your gratitude for what this facilitates, you are more likely to be able to continue with it. In all of this you set an example for your children that when things are difficult, asking for help is a good strategy and one that brings us closer to the people who care about us.

NEXT STEPS

If you are reading this chapter as a parent who has been given a cancer diagnosis, or because someone you care about is in this position, it is hoped that the information above will support you to move forward in a way that is best for you, your children, and those you love. Remember, there is no perfect way to parent. Protecting our children often means teaching them how to deal with life's painful moments rather than trying to hide painful realities from them. Taking the time to think about what you need and to share your worries and concerns with people who can support you is the first step towards being able to talk to your children about your cancer diagnosis.

By being open with them, in a way that they can understand, you are letting your children know that yes, difficult things happen, but that as a family you can talk about them, comfort each other and find a way to still be ok.

ADDITIONAL RESOURCES

Resources for Parents
General information about talking to children
Irish Cancer Society www.cancer.ie/sites/default/files/2019-11/talking_to_children_2017.pdf
Cancer Council, New South Wales, Australia www.cancercouncil.com.au/cancer-information/for-family-and-friends/talking-to-kids-about-cancer/
Cancer Research UK www.cancerresearchuk.org/about-cancer/coping/emotionally/support-for-children-whose-parents-have-cancer

Resources for Children
Dana Farber Cancer Institute have produced YouTube videos aimed at children and teens whose parents have a diagnosis www.dana-farber.org/for-patients-and-families/care-and-treatment/support-services-and-amenities/family-connections/

The National Cancer Institute in America has a booklet for called 'When your parent has cancer – a guide for teens'. This gives tips and ideas on how to talk about cancer and how it may affect the family www.cancer.gov/publications/patient-education/when-your-parent-has-cancer

CHAPTER 12

Survivorship: Living with and beyond cancer

Natalie Hession

This chapter aims to broadly focus on survivorship and what that can look like and how it is understood by some people. For many the fear of recurrence is a major emotional challenge that typically increases with certain events such as scan results or the illness of a loved one. It is common and completely normal to be concerned about whether the cancer will come back. When treatment ends you may expect life to return to the way it was before you were diagnosed with cancer, but it will take time to recover. You may have permanent scars or you may not be able to do some things you once found easy. You may also have emotional scars from going through so much.

In this chapter we will also look at family relationships. We will cover family relationships and how to manage the possible change and adjustment to these relationships post treatment. Every family is different and how each member deals with cancer in the family is different. We will discuss returning to work: when to return and certain challenges that could possibly arise, and suggestions that you could reflect on to assist you in this transition. Most people will come face to face with the fear of recurrence, deal with how survivorship may impact your family and the challenges of returning to work. Despite these challenges being difficult, they are normal. This chapter is not intended to be an instruction as to how to do this, but it will highlight some of the issues and challenges that one can face whilst living with and beyond your cancer diagnosis.

SURVIVORSHIP: LIVING WITH AND BEYOND CANCER

Over the past few years there has been a significant shift in cancer care, from 'curing' to 'living well' during and after a cancer diagnosis. As a result many millions of people across the world are living with and beyond cancer. The term 'survivorship' is used to refer to anyone who has been diagnosed with cancer, from the time of diagnosis through the rest of his or her life. You may not like the term, or you may feel that it does not apply to you. The word 'survivorship' helps many people think about embracing their lives living with and beyond their cancer diagnosis. However, survivorship is a very personal thing and something that can be defined only by you, as you consider your unique personal feelings and life goals. Each person diagnosed with cancer will have their own, very personal definition of survivorship; and each person is unique in how they deal with survivorship. In general terms, a large component of 'surviving' cancer has to do with being in control of one's life as much *as possible*, and with being as 'well' *as possible*, and with finding joy and pleasure in living life to the fullest extent *as possible*.

It is estimated that 25 per cent of individuals will have one or more physical or psychological consequences following their cancer treatment that affects their life to a greater or lesser degree in the long term. For many, long-term side effects of cancer treatment can negatively impact on their psychological (such as low mood or anxiety), physical (such as long-term side effects of treatment) and social (such as impact on sexual relationships) wellbeing. Ultimately this may have a detrimental impact on their quality of life.

Living with and beyond cancer may mean adjusting to a loss and change in life roles and aspirations. You may experience changes that are very different from someone else's, even if that person had the same type of cancer and treatment as you. For some, life after a cancer diagnosis may be like a roller coaster ride: moments when you feel like you can handle all the stress and moments when you feel overwhelmed; hours when life looks richer and brighter than ever before, and hours when all the world appears gloomy; times when you are brimming with confidence and optimism, and times when you want to give up. Despite how challenging this may be, it is normal.

FEAR OF RECURRENCE: LET ME LIVE MY LIFE

One of the hardest things after treatment is not knowing what happens next. It can be a time of uncertainty and you may ask yourself many questions: 'Will I be fit to return to work?', 'Will I ever gain my confidence again?', 'Will my cancer return?' Fear of recurrence is normal and often lessens over time. However, even years after treatment, some events may cause you to become worried about recurrence. Follow-up appointments, certain symptoms, the illness of a loved one, or the anniversary date of when you were first diagnosed can all trigger concern and worries about recurrence. One way to think about worry and anxiety is that being worried or anxious highlights the things you value dearly, and it shows your courage in facing up to the things that appear threatened by cancer.

Things to consider that may help you to cope with your fears:

Keep note of concerns to inform medical team

Following treatment, it is very common to have fears about every ache and pain. Talk to your medical team if you are having a symptom that worries you. Just having a conversation with them about your symptoms may help calm your fears and, over time, you may start to recognise certain feelings in your body as normal. Keep notes about any symptoms you have. Write down questions for your medical team before follow-up appointments so you can be prepared to tell them what you have been going through since your last appointment. Be honest about the fears of your cancer coming back so the medical team can address your worries. Everyone's cancer is different, as is the risk of recurrence.

Be informed

Understand what you can do for your health now, and find out about the services that are available to you such as local Irish Cancer Society support centres. Cancer support centres typically host various programmes to help with your emotional and physical well-being such as stress management programmes, gentle yoga, art classes, talks and so on. Getting involved in these activities may give you a greater sense of control over your well-being. Be mindful of the worry and anxiety that searching on the internet for information related to your symptoms and cancer type can often lead to. As opposed to reducing worry and anxiety, it can often create more. Try to stick to the information and literature your medical team gives you and prioritise searching on reputable websites such as the Irish Cancer Society's website. Your medical team can give you the facts about your type of cancer and the chances of recurrence. They can assure you that they are looking out for you.

Develop a follow-up care plan

A follow up or survivorship care plan is a record and a convenient way to store information about your cancer and treatment history, as well as any check-ups or follow-up tests you need in the future. It may also list possible long-term effects of your treatments, and ideas for staying healthy. Having a plan may give you a sense of control and allow you to manage your health. Suggestions of survivorship care plan templates can be found at the following websites:

https://www.cancer.net/survivorship/follow-care-after-cancer-treatment
http://mncanceralliance.org/wp-content/uploads/2013/07/SurvivorCarePlan
3202012_Final.pdf

Begin to notice and accept your feelings

It is completely normal to be experiencing a wide range of emotions including worry. Attempting to allow your feelings to be and not trying to change your feelings is an important first step to building resilience. The simple act of naming your emotions has been found to be beneficial. So, take a moment to tune into your body and notice how you are feeling. Remember, it is normal and okay to feel discomfort when you notice certain emotions. Sometimes it is difficult to think of words of comfort for ourselves. Perhaps a helpful way to conjure up kind words towards yourself is to think about what you would say to a young child who was in distress or was worried. You could say to them, 'yes, this is difficult but you are doing okay'. These are the same words you may use towards yourself when feelings of discomfort arise as you notice certain emotions.

Attempt to redirect worries

If you are aware that you have increased hypothetical worry (i.e., the 'what if?' thoughts), you may find it helpful to practice noticing these thoughts and then redirecting your attention to things within your control. Research shows that when we shift our focus to what we can control, we see meaningful and lasting differences in our wellbeing. For example, if you were worried about the outcome of a follow up scan, you may ask yourself: 'Is this concern within my own control or not?' If not, the next question maybe, 'Is it helpful or beneficial to me to worry about this?'. If the answer is 'no', the next question could be 'What is under my control?', and the answer to this could be 'to begin/continue to look after my emotional well-being and to follow any after treatment care as mentioned to me by my medical team'.

Talk to a psychologist or counsellor
If you find that the fear of recurrence is more than you can handle, ask your medical team/GP for a referral for someone to talk to. If you find it difficult to engage in everyday activities or the thoughts about cancer recurrence are keeping you awake at night, you might feel better meeting with a psychologist or counsellor working in the area of cancer care.

Balance how much attention to give cancer
How much attention to give cancer is a dilemma. On the one hand, it is good in principle to give aches and pains the attention they deserve. On the other hand, it is good not to be preoccupied with it. It is important to keep this attention you give cancer in its place so it does not take over your life. The solution to this dilemma, of course, is balance. However, achieving this balance is difficult and an ongoing process. You may find yourself consumed with cancer thoughts. You may ask yourself, 'Am I allowing time for other things in my life?', 'Is it helping me thinking about cancer this much?'. On the other hand, you may ask yourself, 'have I ignored my physical symptoms for sometime?', 'am I ignoring my symptoms out of fear of further investigations or treatments?'.

FAMILY AFTER TREATMENT: FIGURING OUT FAMILY RELATIONSHIPS WHEN TREATMENT ENDS

When treatment ends, families (be it those you live with or extended family) are often unprepared for the fact that your recovery takes time, that you will not bounce back to your old self once the treatment is over. Following treatment people often say that they did not realise how much time they needed to recover. This can lead to disappointment, worry and frustration for everyone.

Unfortunately, for some families, problems that were present before the cancer diagnosis may very likely still be there or new ones may develop after treatment has finished. Although treatment has ended, you may still need to receive support and yet people may expect you to do what you did before you were diagnosed. For example, if you used to take care of the house before your treatment, you may find that these jobs are still too much for you to handle. Family members who took over for you may want life to go back to normal. They may expect you to do what you used to do around the house. They may disappoint you, which might make you feel let down, angry or frustrated. Perhaps you do not look unwell and as a result you may get less concern than you did during treatment. It can be complex: you may want family life to be back to normal as it was prior to diagnosis, at the same time you may want your family to support you more or as they did during treatment.

Here are some ideas that have helped others deal with family concerns:

- Know that this is a new time in your life so it may take time to adjust. Roles in the family may change again and different emotions may get triggered. This is normal.
- Family members are not mind-readers. It is best to take the lead in letting them know what you need practically and emotionally. You may say, 'They should just know'. However, your needs may change from day to day and even moment to moment, and your family needs guidance.
- Let your family know what you are able to do as you recover and what not to expect. For example, do not feel like you have to keep the house in perfect order because you always did in the past. Pause and take note of what is important now in order to help you prioritise.
- Exploring and coming to understand your emotions can enable you to communicate with family more fully. Alongside this, you could consider sharing the meaning of your cancer experience with your loved ones. When your loved ones understand how you feel and why you are feeling that way, you will feel less isolated and less emotionally alone. Seeking outside help is also ok if these feelings of isolation still remain i.e., if feelings of loneliness and isolation are constant, difficult to put aside and are leading to low mood.
- For some, asking for help is difficult. In particular for those that have always been the carer/the main earner. Accepting help may feel like a loss of identity and purpose. It may bring thoughts of feeling like a burden. Good communication such as being open with each other can help ensure that each person's needs are met. In this way, you are more likely to get the support you need, and your loved ones will feel helpful.
- At the same time you are going through this experience, your family is adjusting too. It may be hard for all of you to express feelings or know how to talk about cancer. Families also may not realise that the way your family interacts and the roles each play may have changed permanently as a result of cancer. They may need help dealing with the changes and keeping the 'new' family strong. Please refer to the general resource section ahead for booklets that may be helpful for family members.
- If there are children in your family, help them understand that it may take a while for you to have the energy you used to have now that you are finished with treatment. Be open about what you can and cannot do. You do not have

to tell your kids about every follow up appointment or every symptom that occurs. But do tell them if you still have side effects that make certain things hard for you to do. If you are not able to do an activity or go to an event, the children may think that you are unhappy with them. Chapter eleven explores the topic of children in more detail.

- Finally, give yourself time. You and your family will be able to adjust over time to the changes cancer brings.

RETURNING TO WORK: WHEN IS THE RIGHT TIME?

When to return to work is often a difficult question to answer. In making this decision you will need to consider any financial pressures you have. In addition consider whether you have adequate energy levels to sustain the working day/week, and if you feel in a good place emotionally to be able to manage the extra emotional pressures that work can often bring. Be mindful that returning to work too soon can possibly result in having to take time off work again. This could occur if you return to a full working week immediately and come to the realisation that you cannot manage a full week due to fatigue, pain or feeling emotionally overwhelmed.

Points to consider when returning to work

- Start by speaking informally to your supervisor/manager, human resources office or employee assistance counsellor. If necessary, ask for a change that would make it easier for you to do your job (for example, flexitime, working at home, special equipment at work). If required, you could ask your medical team to write a letter to your employer explaining how, if at all, your cancer may affect your work or your schedule.
- If possible keep up contacts during your recovery as this will allow for an easier transition back to work. Work colleagues may worry about you, however, if they find out about your treatment and progress, they will be less anxious and scared. Talk to them on the phone, send email, or if you are fatigued ask a trusted friend or family member to do this for you. When you are able, maybe have lunch with work colleagues. Your return to work will likely be easier for you and others if you stay in touch.
- Plan what you will say about your cancer to your colleagues. It may be helpful to rehearse some answers to possible questions before returning to work. In particular, if there are certain questions that evoke some emotion, you may consider having a stock reply. For some people they do not want to focus on their cancer or be linked in people's minds with the disease. Others are very open about it, speaking frankly with their boss or other workers to air concerns

and correct incorrect ideas. The best approach is the one that feels right for you.

- The response of work colleagues may differ. Some may be a huge source of support, while others may be a source of anger or frustration. Some people mean well, but they do not know the right thing to say. Maybe they just do not know how to offer support or they may feel uncomfortable speaking about cancer. If work colleagues seem unsupportive, it could be because they are anxious for you or for themselves. Your cancer experience may threaten them because it reminds them that cancer can happen to anyone. Many say that acting cheerful around others, including work colleagues, for their comfort is a strain. One person post treatment noted, 'I don't have the energy to be upbeat all the time.' As you sort out what matters most, you may even decide to let some colleague friendships go, to give more time to the meaningful ones.

- Address any problems that come up when you go back to work. Your manager or work colleagues may be able to help those around you understand how you want to be treated. If problems with others get in the way of your work, you may want to talk with your manager, your union or the company's human resources department. Do not be afraid to ask, even if it has been some time since you returned to work.

CONCLUSION

The end of treatment can be a time to look forward to the future. You are probably relieved to be finished with the demands of treatment and are ready to put the experience behind you. Yet at the same time, you may feel sad and worried. For many the fear of recurrence is a major emotional challenge. Some say that although they were relieved when treatment ended, it was hard to transition to a new way of life. It is not so much 'getting back to normal' as it is finding out what is normal for you now. This new normal may come with changes to family relationships as well as challenges related to returning to work. It is impossible to eliminate all the unpleasant emotions, discomforts, worries and uncertainties. Whatever your new normal may be, give yourself time to adapt to the changes. Allow time for you and your family members and caregivers to adjust and make sense of your individual experiences. Whether good or bad, life-changing situations often give people the chance to grow, learn, and appreciate what is important to them. People often say that life has new meaning or that they look at things differently following their cancer. Some describe it as being like entering another world where they had to adjust to new feelings, new challenges, changes in support, and different ways of looking at the world. You may see yourself in a different way or find that others think of you differently now. You are still you: doing the best you can in difficult times.

ADDITIONAL RESOURCES

Book:
Kate Lorig et al., *Self-Management of Long-Term Health Conditions* (Colorado, 2014)

Websites:
Suggestions of survivorship care plan templates can be found at the following websites
www.cancer.net/survivorship/follow-care-after-cancer-treatment
mncanceralliance.org/wp-content/uploads/2013/07/SurvivorCarePlan3202012_Final.pdf

CHAPTER 13

Living with uncertainty: Living with incurable cancer

David Shannon

If you are reading this chapter, it is likely you have received news that your cancer is no longer curable. This chapter is intended to offer you support and guidance in living fully and well – not despite your cancer being no longer curable but because of it. Learning that your cancer is no longer curable is an important milestone in your cancer journey. Maybe you already had a sense of this before hearing the news from your doctors or perhaps you had hoped for further treatment. This may also have come as a complete shock to you. As a result of this news, you may find yourself feeling lost or experiencing a range of emotions from fear and sadness to anxiety, loneliness, or anger.

Although cure of the disease is no longer possible, the focus of your care now will most likely turn to helping you manage any difficult symptoms you may have. These can include tiredness, pain, sickness or anxiety. You may hear your medical team talk about helping you have the best possible quality of life, given your type of cancer. It takes time to adjust to treatment ending and what this means. You will most likely want to know how much time you have left. Your medical team may have already spoken with you about this. Generally, it is very difficult to give an exact timeframe beyond guidelines of weeks, months or sometimes longer. Usually, it will depend on the type of cancer you have and where it is in your body.

This uncertainty is often one of the most stressful parts of the end of treatment. It is very common to feel more anxious or fearful as a result of not knowing for certain how much time you have left. Thoughts of time is a very common kind of 'trap' to get caught in when treatment ends. This is discussed further below. This chapter is written in the context of a rapidly changing cultural backdrop in Ireland. Over recent years many developments have opened the country to a welcome set of new and diverse cultural perspectives and religious practices. Historically, the specialty of hospice and end-of-life care in Ireland has been strongly influenced by Catholic religious orders. This has changed radically in recent decades to reflect Ireland's changing cultural and religious landscape. Although this chapter offers primarily a secular/non-religious perspective on adapting to end-of-life, this is not to undervalue the depth and solace offered by different cultural traditions and religious practices that are now available in Ireland.

DEATH AND DYING: THE 'ELEPHANT' IN THE ROOM

It is difficult to talk about death. This seems especially so today, when facing death can seem like a personal failure, almost as if it is something to be ashamed of or embarrassed about. Dying is the natural way all life comes to an end. It may seem like a failure if the body has not been able to cope with the demands placed on it by medical treatments, such as chemotherapy. Feelings of failure may also be fuelled by feeling like a burden due to the impact your illness is having on those closest to you. Although such feelings are very common, feeling that you are somehow responsible for the failure of your treatment, is never helpful and not true. Remember medicine and the body have their limits.

WHAT DOES DYING LOOK LIKE?

Dying does not suddenly begin when treatment ends. Living and dying take place side by side all the time. Cells in the body are constantly dying and new cells take their place. This happens from the time we are born. The dying that comes with end of life is usually recognisable in advance – if we know what to look for. Dying from different types of cancer often includes increased tiredness and more prolonged periods of sleeping. Your palliative care team is expert in managing the symptoms associated with dying. If you choose, it may be helpful to talk with them about how dying is likely to look like in someone with your type of cancer.

Although this can be a difficult conversation, it will allow your medical team to reassure you about the supports and medication they can offer you to help relieve any symptoms you may be worried about. Without this information, you may mistakenly think that some symptoms you are experiencing mean that you are dying, when in fact it may be a symptom of the disease that can be treated. Usually, the earlier your doctor knows about your symptoms, the better they can help you to manage them.

FOCUSING ON WHAT YOU CAN CONTROL, LETTING GO OF WHAT YOU CANNOT

A feeling of loss of control is one of the most common and understandable feelings that arise as a result of knowing your disease cannot be cured. However, control is never 'all-or-nothing'. Even though you may not be able to control what the disease does, there are still many things you do have control over. It is especially important at a time like this to focus on what you can control, even though you will most likely continue to dwell on what you cannot. If you can keep focusing on the things that you can control, this will help to reduce your anxiety in relation to things which you cannot. Engaging in regular periods of relaxation can also be especially helpful when feeling anxious. Making choices about spending time with people, doing things you most enjoy and in places you feel most relaxed can be a nourishing way to take care of yourself. These choices will be unique to you. For one person, time alone is nourishing, for another, it is spending time with others. There is no one right way.

Another way to take control is to plan ahead. The Irish Hospice Foundation (IHF) has produced a very helpful document entitled, 'Think Ahead' which can guide you through making important decisions around healthcare planning and thinking through your wishes should you become unable to. The 'Think Ahead' document combines questions around your healthcare plan, financial planning, specific cultural and religious practices, as well as arrangements following death. A link to this document is given at the end of this chapter and in the Additional Resources section at the end of the book.

FEELINGS ARE LIKE THE WEATHER

Feelings are a good example of something we cannot control. Feelings are like the weather. We would never try to control the weather, yet in many ways our feelings are like our own internal weather system. Perhaps the best we can do in bad weather, like in a storm, is to take care and allow it to pass. The more we try to change what is happening or how we are feeling, the more we are likely to make things worse. For example, if we are feeling sad, forcing ourselves to feel happy or 'positive' will most likely just make us feel worse, as it is putting added pressure on ourselves not to feel the way we are feeling.

It is at times like this that we learn we are not in control – the weather is. Feelings and emotions are much like this. We need to take care and allow them to pass. What we can control is what we do while waiting for the bad weather/feeling/mood to pass. This might include talking to family and friends, spending time in nature and taking care of the body with rest, exercise and nourishing food.

PRACTICAL ARRANGEMENTS – YOUR WILL AND FUNERAL

One area you may find yourself thinking about are practical issues, like making a Will and making funeral arrangements. These may weigh on your mind and can often cause anxiety and stress until they are dealt with. These are things you can control. Once you attend to practical matters such as making a Will you may feel a great sense of relief that it is done. It will also be something you no longer need to worry about. This should help to free up some 'headspace' and at the same time allow you to gain a sense of control over what is happening. Talking to someone about funeral arrange-ments is another practical thing that will likely make you feel more at ease once it has been done. Otherwise, it may continue to pop into your mind as another thing you have to do and so may end up increasing your sense of stress. Again, the Irish Hospice Foundation's 'Think Ahead' document may be a useful place to start in having these conversations.

The more attention you can give to these matters when you are relatively well, the more you can then let go of them, as there may come a time when it is too late to give them the time and attention they deserve. Attending to practical matters such as your funeral wishes and Will also means that your family does not have to worry about them. So, this is also a way for you to take care of them, knowing this will help to ease their stress as well.

INFORMATION AND ACCEPTING HELP

Another way of taking control is to decide what medical information you would like to have. You can decide what questions to ask about your illness and how it will be handled now that treatment has come to an end. For example, you may have questions about how different symptoms will be managed, or how the dying process itself is likely to be. If so, asking questions and getting the information you need may help you to feel less anxious and more in control. Usually, if there is something we do not know, we 'fill in the blanks' with what we imagine to be true but may not be. This is often the case when it comes to the dying process. In this way, seeking information from your doctors and asking questions can often be settling and reassuring.

Your family and friends will naturally be very concerned about you over the coming weeks and months and will almost certainly be keeping a very close eye on you. At times this might feel claustrophobic. For example, they may want to do more for you than you need, or insist you let them do things for you that you can do for yourself. There may be a balance to be struck here, as allowing others to help you and be a part of your life at this time is actually a precious gift you can give them.

THE PROBLEM WITH FOCUSING ON TIME

Even though your cancer may no longer be curable what is often unknown is how much time is left. This uncertainty is often very stressful, as it can bring fear and thoughts of a loss of control to the fore. It is common for the mind to get 'stuck' focusing on time, especially when cure is no longer possible. A common thought may be something like, 'If cure is no longer possible and no one can tell me how long I have left to live, what is there left to live for?' Seen psychologically, this could be viewed as an understandable attempt to remain in control. However, it is at times like this that it can be helpful to remember once again that control is not an 'all or nothing' affair. Giving too much attention to thinking about time can ironically rob you of much of the time you actually do have. As mentioned above, there are still many things you could direct your attention to instead, such as enjoying nature or choosing to be with family and friends. Another common thought is, 'If I could just know how much time is left, I could live my life as normal and only tend to my affairs and say my goodbyes when I really need to, right at the very end.' The natural grief we will all feel at the end of life is not easy, so it is no wonder that we would procrastinate or seek to delay or avoid preparing for death until absolutely necessary.

In coming to terms with the end of life, we will all naturally grieve and feel sad. It is important to understand that this is normal. However, sadness is not the only emotion we will likely feel. Grief is characterised by a range of emotions – guilt, anger, appreciation, relief, anxiety, connection. If you can allow yourself to feel however you are feeling, the less stressed you are going to feel, and the more you will be in sync with what is happening. As the Canadian writer Stephen Jenkinson has observed, grief can perhaps more accurately and helpfully be thought of as a skill, as something that can be learned and practiced.

THE PROBLEM WITH FOCUSING ON SYMPTOMS

It is understandable that worrying about troublesome symptoms such as pain, nausea or fatigue might occupy a lot of your time, energy and attention. For example, it is common to associate pain with dying. However, it is important to remember that pain is not the same as dying. The two are not related. Increasing pain does not mean that death is getting closer. It may be helpful to track your symptoms and record times of the day/night when your symptoms are better/worse. This information can be very helpful for your medical team who can help you address symptoms such as pain through medication or other medical procedures and improve your quality of life.

Sometimes it may be helpful to ask yourself what the worst part of a particular symptom (e.g., pain, fatigue, nausea) is? Might it be possible to address this? For example, if sickness is preventing you from eating, what is the worst part about this? Does it mean you cannot be around food or be with family at mealtimes? Does this then have a knock-on effect of making you feel more alone? If so, might there still be ways to stay involved and connected to others at mealtimes even though you are not eating?

APPRECIATION AND DISTRACTION

Focusing solely on managing difficult symptoms may mean that you miss out on or forget about other important aspects of your life, such as appreciating your relationships with loved ones, spending time in nature or considering the life you have led and especially those aspects of your life that you are most proud of. Sometimes you might find activity helps to distract you from focusing on difficult symptoms. This might be something as simple as having a phone-call with a friend or spending time on a hobby, light housework or appreciating nature.

MANAGING YOUR ENERGY AND ACCEPTING LIMITATIONS

Or perhaps you are trying to manage your energy levels and find yourself sleeping more. Might it be possible to pace yourself throughout the day, arranging to do things or meet people at those times in the day when your energy is best? Can you build-in regular periods of rest? Sometimes this will also mean adjusting what you or others expect of you. There may be very real limitations to what you can do as illness progresses, so it will be important to allow for this. Speaking with family and friends about what you are/are not able to do may also be helpful. This is often the most frustrating part of living with advanced incurable illness. The more you can begin to accept these limitations (once medicine has offered all it can to help), the more at ease you will feel.

STAYING CONNECTED

Due to the effects of illness, you may have stopped socialising, going shopping or visiting favourite places. It is important to remember that activity and socialising are vital for our mood. This is especially true if you are living with advanced illness. Maybe you need to be near a toilet in case you need to use it urgently. For this reason, you may have stopped going out altogether. Sharing such concerns with family and working out together if there might be ways around these kinds of obstacles (e.g., bringing spare pads and a change of clothes), may help you to maintain such activities. There may come a time when it truly becomes impossible for you to leave the house, but you may not have reached this point yet. Often careful planning and a willingness to be open and share with family members the obstacles you are facing can help to overcome them. Finding ways to continue to do the things you love can help living with advanced illness. Allowing your family to assist you with these struggles will also be very helpful and meaningful for them.

LIVING YOUR VALUES AND FOCUSING ON WHAT MATTERS

Instead of focusing on time or symptoms, another option always available to you is to focus on what matters most to you or on what makes life worthwhile. For many of us this will be spending time with family, friends, around animals, or in nature. Long-held interests or hobbies, as well as spending time in places you enjoy (this may simply be at home or in the garden) can also be very therapeutic.

Our mood gets enormous benefits from planning, even if our plans need to change at the last minute. Some activities may require careful planning as you may not be able to know for sure if you will have the energy to do them. However, it is nearly always worth planning them regardless. The danger is you may stop planning anything at all, which can lower our mood. This can result in feeling lonelier and more isolated at precisely the time in your life when you might benefit most from these kinds of activities. Focusing on what is most important and putting your energy and attention into these (to whatever extent possible) means that you will be living your values. The final chapter in this book develops this theme further.

THE ROLE OF MINDFULNESS IN TAKING CARE

Mindfulness meditation is a mind-body practice you may have heard of, which some people find helpful when living with advanced illness. The final chapter in this book explains some aspects of this approach – 'getting present' – that you may find particularly helpful. Mindfulness also means taking care and being kind to yourself, no matter what you may be facing. This can be challenging, as it is often much easier to be kinder to others than to ourselves. Resources for practicing mindfulness are given at the end of this chapter.

SUMMARY

Grief is a natural part of adjusting to end of life and knowing your cancer is incurable. Simply allowing yourself to feel what you are feeling is often a good first step in managing difficult feelings. It is especially important to allow for the sadness that is a part of grief. Talking with family and friends about how you are feeling is often a helpful way of making sense of what is happening. Talking can allow you to 'hear yourself' as you begin to make sense of things. This can help to prioritise what is most important, as often this becomes clearer as we begin speaking about things.

Sometimes talking with a health professional attached to your medical team can be a good stepping-stone to speaking with loved ones. If you find yourself feeling very stuck or very sad, activity and spending time on pleasurable activities often helps. Spending time with people or in places where you feel relaxed and at ease can also be helpful when feeling anxious. Being clear on what you can and cannot control and focusing on what you can will help you to feel better. This is also likely to help those around you at the same time, as they will feel reassured when they know you are looking after yourself.

ADDITIONAL RESOURCES

Books and Audio Books:
Jon Kabat-Zinn, *Mindfulness for Beginners: Reclaiming the Present Moment and Your Life* (Colorado, 2016) Available in all formats, including audiobook.

Mark G. Williams and Danny Penman, *Mindfulness: A Practical guide to Finding Peace in a Frantic World* (London, 2011). Available in all formats, including audiobook

Websites:
The Irish Hospice Foundation, Think Ahead Document hospicefoundation.ie/wp-content/uploads/2021/06/Think_Ahead_Editable-for-web.pdf

CHAPTER 14

Knowing what matters most

Louise McHugh

When someone gets a cancer diagnosis they do not expect it, they do not like it, and they definitely do not want it; and, unfortunately, the diagnosis is just the beginning. From receiving the diagnosis to managing treatment and the side effects there is a lot to process along the way. Painful emotions will come up for us: fear, disappointment, envy, jealousy, shock, grief, sadness, anger, anxiety, outrage, dread, guilt, resentment; perhaps even hatred, despair or disgust. Most of us do not know how to deal with such difficult emotions. This is because our society does not teach us how to handle such challenges. More specifically, it does not teach us how to handle them effectively. In this chapter we want to look at ways we can cope with and feel fulfilled in the face of the most difficult challenges that life throws at us.

Two skills that have been shown to promote well-being and help us cope with difficult life experiences are purpose and getting present. Purpose is our hearts desire for who we want to be and how we want to be as a human. Getting present is about coming out of automatic pilot. We spend much of our lives just moving from one thing to the next. We live out our daily routines without reflecting on them. We get up, eat our breakfast, and get about our daily tasks on automatic pilot. When we learn to come out of auto pilot we notice things that we did not pay attention to before. Often the things we do not pay attention to are not just trivial but important things that matter in our lives. In this chapter we are going to introduce the skills of purpose and getting present, and how they can help you face coping with cancer.

PURPOSE

My mother was diagnosed with leukemia when I was 16 years old. She died six weeks later, on Christmas day. During those six weeks a diamond fell out of her engagement ring. My father went to great lengths to get it fixed before she died. I mention this story because there was a fundamental moment in my life that happened around that event. I arrived to visit my mother in hospital. My father was already in the room as I peeked in the door. I overheard their conversation. My father pulled out the fixed ring and said 'If you had the chance would you do it all again?' and she nodded. It struck me that in the end that is all that really matters: living a life of purpose that you would do again because it was a life that was filled with doing what mattered to you. We want to live a life that we would 'do again'. For this to be the case it is important that we know what truly matters to us. This allows us to consciously choose to do the things that we care about rather than going about our daily routine on automatic pilot.

At times of difficulty such as coping with all stages of cancer there is an opportunity in the shock and terrible situation to ask ourselves some big questions such as 'What really matters to me deep down?'; 'What do I want my life to stand for?'; 'What type of person do I want to be in the face of this?' As you read those questions you may realise you have not spent much time thinking about these types of things before.

If you find yourself new to these questions one way to get started can be to think of the opposite. To do that, I invite you to think about a person in the public eye who lives their life the exact opposite of how you want to live yours. Give yourself a couple of minutes to select someone. Now list three things about the way they are that you would not like to be. For example, selfish, disconnected and intolerant would be ones that come to mind for the person I selected. I invite you to think about what is the opposite of each of these descriptions from your perspective. For me the opposite of selfish is kind, the opposite of disconnected is connected, and the opposite of intolerant is compassionate. These opposites can give you an insight into how you want to be in the world.

Connecting to our purpose gives our lives direction. The descriptions above are qualities we can always bring to our lives. At any given time I can set my intention to be kind, connected and compassionate. Notice that these are not specific goals. When we connect to our purpose it is useful to set goals but first we need to be clear on the qualities we want to bring. These can act as guides whenever we have a difficult decision to make. At any given time if faced with a decision where I am unsure about what I want to do, and what goals I want to set for myself, I can use my values as a guide. Right now I am writing this chapter, and when I think of my value of connection, a goal I can set for myself is to spend an hour each day writing so as to complete the chapter and connect to you the readers about strategies to make coping with life's challenges easier. When we do not connect to our purpose we can spend our lives just doing things we 'should be doing' rather than really reflecting on what we value doing. When we are going through life in this way we can feel empty, wondering why we do not feel more fulfilled.

When my stepmother had breast cancer it really shocked her to the core. She had always believed she would live forever. At that time on reflecting and asking herself some really hard questions about what mattered to her she realised that contribution – helping her community and making a difference – was something that really mattered to her. She decided that raising funds to support research into breast cancer to help other people who would have to go through what she went through was one way for her to live that value of contribution. She brought together a group of people and set up Mayo Pink Ribbon, a charity that hosts an annual fund-raising cycle to fund breast cancer research at the National University of Ireland, Galway. This has been ongoing for a decade now and they have raised over one million euro for breast cancer research.

Given the fact that being clear on our purpose helps us live a life that matters, why then do we not always take the time to think about our purpose? There are a couple of reasons for this. The first big reason is that society does not often ask us to reflect on what matters to us. The other tricky reason is that when we reflect on and identify our purpose, the gap between where our lives currently are and where we want them to be becomes apparent. In a sense our purpose always holds vulnerability because what we truly care about we also care about not doing or losing.

To illustrate the latter point let us look at an example. I really care about getting science out to the public (i.e., scientific dissemination), and writing is a part of that. At times when I have procrastinated or not written for a few weeks acknowledging that dissemination of science is important to me brings up feelings of discomfort, disappointment and regret. In that sense acknowledging and sharing what matters also brings any lacking between who and how we want to be to the surface. It is unlikely that any of us will be living and being the person we want to be all of the time. I certainly have not met anyone yet who manages to do that. We are human. We will have failed, made mistakes, hurt ourselves and others.

Sometimes people worry that being kind to ourselves when we fail is overly indulgent or that it will stop us being motivated to do better in the future. Actually when we look at the research, people who are kinder to themselves around their mistakes and failings are less likely to repeat these mistakes. Being overly critical with ourselves can make it painful to look at our mistakes and stop us noticing important things. It can stop us noticing that in the future we want to do something different. If we cannot make space for our past mistakes and we try to avoid acknowledging them, it will be hard for us to truly acknowledge what matters to us.

LOSS OF PURPOSE

A dear friend of mine, Siobhan, on receiving a diagnosis of cancer told me she felt hopeless and could not see the point of anything. In her despair she went for a walk in the Wicklow mountains. She told me of how walking around surrounded by the stunning landscape she remembered how much she loved nature and its beauty. She decided that spending time in nature during this difficult time reconnected her to what matters. What Siobhan experienced was something that is often experienced when faced with the tremendously difficult challenge of a cancer diagnosis. Coping with this can shake someone's core in terms of what their purpose is or their understanding of what the meaning of life is. A gentle way to orient ourselves can be to connect to a time when there was some pleasure or joy in our life. Picking even the simplest moment such as seeing a beautiful landscape or holding a baby. When we gently bring to mind a moment of joy that we previously experienced it can tell us something important about what matters to us, just as had happened to Siobhan.

GETTING PRESENT

One thing that helps us notice when we are living our lives on auto pilot and not connecting to our purpose is learning skills to get present to the current moment. In the words of Jon Kabat-Zinn 'Like it or not, this moment is all we really have to work with'. Getting present is about coming out of auto pilot and tuning into your thoughts, feelings and physical sensations in your body as they come and go. Our minds can take us out of the present moment very easily. Even now you might notice as you have been reading this chapter that you thought about lots of other things from as simple to what you will have for dinner tonight to more compelling thoughts about how you are coping in life. We can spend much of our time worrying about a future event that might never happen or over thinking a past event that is long since over.

We may not notice but our minds are thinking all the time. Just pause for a minute and notice what thoughts you are having. Examples of thoughts might be 'This is a strange thing to do!', 'I'm not sure I am doing this right', 'What will I have for dinner?' Starting to notice our mind in this way will help us to notice when our mind is being helpful and also when it is being unhelpful. For example, our mind can be helpful when it is telling us things like 'I am hungry' as that lets us know we should eat. It is not so helpful when it is telling us things like 'I can't bear this' as this might pull us down a spiral of thoughts that takes us away from what matters. We can spend a lot of our time caught up in our minds. And our minds play tricks on us.

A friend of mine has a unique green retro Mercedes. I was going to their house for the first time. I was looking for number 38 along their road. When the satellite navigation did not have a 38 I thought that was unusual. I got to 36 and saw a green Mercedes in the driveway and thought that this is a coincidence but 'where is number 38?'. I walked up and down the road and eventually rang my friend to say that I could not find number 38. His house was number 36 but somehow I latched onto the wrong information (i.e., the house was number 38) and even though all other information in the environment was indicating to me that I was wrong, I did not notice all those cues. What our minds tell us is not always right: our minds can feed us wrong information all the time and yet we believe it and often ignore evidence to the contrary. Often we are unaware of what is actually in front of us and overly reliant on what our mind tells us.

In fact it is not only stuff on the outside that our minds distort in this way. Being caught up in our minds can mean we distort what we think on the inside also. This is particularly true in times of trouble and uncertainty: us humans really do not like uncertainty. When faced with uncertain situations a thing most of us do can be to try to think our way to certainty. For example, we might view a situation as worse than it is. Psychologists refer to this as catastrophising. This happens when we believe that if we do not think through the worst-case scenarios that they will happen. Or we might start to think we can fortune tell what is actually going to happen in the future and start to believe our predictions in a superstitious way. The truth is that we do not have a crystal ball and thinking through the worst-case scenarios does not make them more or less likely to occur. Unfortunately, life is uncertain. The best gift we can give ourselves is to learn to be with uncertainty rather than trying to find false ways to impose certainty on the world, ourselves, and what is going to happen.

When times are difficult people often tell us to trust our gut instinct. Indeed our gut instinct is a powerful source of information, However, we can be so out of touch with our experience that we cannot really tune into what that is. When we slow down and get present it is easier to trust in ourselves. One way to slow down and tune into ourselves is to pause and notice right now in this moment three things that you can hear, three things that you can see and three sensations that you can feel. Take a moment to try that now. If we do this regularly in moments that are easy, then we can gradually build up to doing this even at more difficult moments. This practice will help us tune in to what is present as an alternative to the most typical responses to difficult experiences which are ignoring, fighting, struggling with, bargaining with or denying them.

We want to start to be in control of our minds not vice versa. When we are on auto pilot we just take what our mind is saying as true. For example, if I have the thought 'I cannot cope', I believe this thought to be a true reflection of how things are. As we saw in the example above with house number 36 what our minds are telling us is not always true, and often misses important things. A useful alternative to believing every thought that comes into your mind is considering whether any given thought is helpful or not. Imagine I am going on a first date with someone I really like. The thought 'I am not good enough' pops up in my mind. If I believe that thought as true I might cancel the date, but if I reflect on whether the thought is helpful or not I will notice that really it is not a helpful thought. Coming back to purpose really helps here. If I value a connected, intimate relationship, going on that first date is a goal that aligns to that value. Believing the thought that 'I am not good enough' and cancelling the date does not align to that value.

Noticing whether thoughts are helpful or not is particularly important in times when life is really hard as our minds may come up with all sorts of challenging thoughts that could pull us in unhelpful directions such as isolating ourselves, over thinking, catastrophising, etc. Knowing if thoughts are helpful or not can bring us back to noticing what is important. When we are clear on what matters to us, we can connect to whether believing our thoughts as true will bring us closer to living a life that matters or bring us further away. When my mind pulls me into thoughts that are not useful – 'I cannot cope'; 'I am not good enough' – I can develop the skill of just noticing the thought and come back to what is here in the present moment (e.g., 'I am having the thought that I am not good enough, this is not a fact').

Getting present also involves patience with whatever is here in this moment. This means not trying to rush past whatever current feeling is showing up or getting frustrated with ourselves for whatever thoughts and judgements we might be having. Instead we want to learn to patiently be a witness to whatever experiences are present. To do this we can bring a curiosity rather than a refusal to our experiences. For example, when I have anxiety, rather than trying to talk myself out of it, I can be curious about where I am feeling it, what came before it, why I might be having it and notice all the sensations that make up that feeling.

Practicing noticing our experience at any given moment as if we are experiencing it for the first time is a way to cultivate this curious approach to our experiences. We can take any activity and bring this curiosity to it. Achieving this involves doing the activity as if it is the first time you have ever done it. Noticing all the parts of the activity we do not notice when it is something we do all the time. For example, bringing a first-timer's mind to eating food, going for a walk, looking at a painting. We also want to bring that first-timer's mind to whatever shows up, even the emotions we often think we do not want to have (e.g., fear, disappointment, envy, jealousy, shock, grief, sadness, anger, anxiety, outrage, dread, guilt, resentment).

Imagine, you are an art enthusiast and there is a room in your house where you hang your collection of really fine art. Your collection includes magnificent pieces of work from Van Gogh, Rembrandt, Picasso and then your niece gives you a really ugly framed drawing for your birthday and she hangs it with pride on your art wall. You really do not like the painting. Initially, every time you walk into the room you try to avoid the painting; you think it ruins the room and all the other paintings. Then you stop going into the room as the painting is ruining your whole experience. Over time you miss the room and realise there has to be another way. You start to adopt another strategy, that rather than avoid the painting every time you walk into the room you are going to look straight at it before looking at all the others. Over time you notice that you start to be okay with the painting being there because it means when you look at it you get to look at all the other paintings that are there too.

So even though when you get a cancer diagnosis you do not expect it, you do not like it, and you definitely do not want it, even in the face of this adversity we can ask ourselves some crucial questions about what matters to us. What matters to you is not what matters to society, your family, your friends, or anyone else, it is specifically what matters to you. If nobody else was there to judge your choices what would you want to be remembered for? Some of these values may be shared with others but others will be unique to you. And the ways that you want to live, in line with these values, is unique to you also.

As this chapter comes to a close I invite you to take a few moments to get present to your current experience in an honest and kind way and reflect on the following questions: 'What do I value most?'; 'What do I want to be remembered for?'; 'What kind of person do I want to be in the world?'; 'What actions can I take in my life to be that person even in this difficult time?' At this time of uncertainty let us connect to what matters and engage in a life that allows us to say 'If I had the chance, I would do it all again'.

ADDITIONAL RESOURCES

Books:

Russ Harris, *When Life Hits Hard: How to Transcend Grief, Crisis, and Loss with Acceptance and Commitment Therapy* (Oakland, California, 2021)

Steve Hayes, *A Liberated Mind: How to Pivot Toward What Matters* (New York, 2019)

Website:
contextualscience.org

Index

thought loops 22, 36
throat cancer 11
transplants 50
treatment decisions 93
treatments for cancer, generally 13–16, 71
   side effects 62, 71
tricyclic antidepressants (TCAs) 65

vaccination 11–12
   HPV 11
victim blaming 23, 25

viruses 11

wellness plan 54
Williams, M. 75
Williams, Mark G. 130
work, returning to 119–20
World Health Organisation (WHO)
   70

Yalom, Irvin D. 8
yoga 55, 62